صاحب السمو الشيخ زايد بن سلطان آل نهيان رئيس دولة الامارات العربية
المتحدة، حاكم أبو ظبي.

His Highness Sheikh Zayed bin Sultan Al Nahyan,
President of the United Arab Emirates and Ruler of Abu Dhabi.

INTRODUCTION

Many visitors come to Abu Dhabi expecting to find nothing but sand dunes and blue Gulf waters. Instead, they are surprised to find a well-developed city — a city where modernity blends with history and where progress is enhanced by a rich heritage. Abu Dhabi, the capital city of the United Arab Emirates, started as a tiny centre for fishing and pearl diving on a small island separated from the mainland by a narrow waterway. By the early 1970s its inhabited area was less than nine square kilometres with a population of less than 25,000.

Since the 1970s the city has experienced phenomenal growth due to the efforts and hard work of His Highness the President, Sheikh Zayed bin Sultan Al Nahyan. Abu Dhabi now covers the original island, part of the mainland and a number of nearby islands. The inhabited area has grown more than twenty-fold and the population more than ten-fold. Today, Abu Dhabi stands as one of the most important cultural and economic centres in the region.

This book gives a brief description of the major features of the city's history, heritage and progress. Several factors have combined to produce the rich tapestry that is Abu Dhabi. Among these are a long history of continuous human settlement, the discovery of major oil reserves in the 1960s, and the rigorous participation by the indigenous population in navigation and commercial exchange with other trade centres of the Middle East and South Asia. Also, the people of the region played a major role in the transmission of religious ideas and in providing the world with innovative concepts in culture, architecture and the arts. All this has contributed to the development of a genuine heritage which stands as evidence of the uniqueness of the area and its inhabitants.

This new edition seeks to emphasise the commitment of the United Arab Emirates and its leaders to linking the present with the past, thereby building a strong formulation for a prosperous future. Hopefully, this revised edition will stimulate new interest in old as well as new readers as they learn of the history, the folklore and the progress of our beautiful city, Abu Dhabi.

Sheikh Nahyan bin Mubarak Al Nahyan
Minister of Higher Education
United Arab Emirates

تقـــديم

يتوقع كثير من الزوار القادمين الى أبو ظبي ان لا يجدوا فيها غير الكثبان الرملية ومياه الخليج الزرقاء. لكنهم يدهشون عندما يجدوا مدينة متطورة تجمع بين العصرية والعراقة، مدينة ذات تراث أصيل يعزز تقدمها الى الأمام.

نشأت مدينة أبو ظبي، عاصمة الامارات العربية المتحدة، كمركز صغير لصيد السمك واللؤلؤ على جزيرة صغيرة يفصلها عن اليابسة برزخ مائي ضيق. وفي أوائل السبعينيات، لم تكن مساحتها المأهولة تزيد عن ٩ كيلومترات مربعة، فيما كان عدد سكانها يقل عن ٢٥،٠٠٠ نسمة.

إلا ان المدينة شهدت بعد ذلك تطورا أسطوريا بفضل الجهود الكبيرة لصاحب السمو الشيخ زايد بن سلطان آل نهيان، رئيس الدولة. وهي تغطي الآن الجزيرة الاصلية التي نشأت عليها، وجزءا من اليابسة المجاورة وعددا من الجزر القريبة. وقد تضاعفت مساحتها المأهولة أكثر من عشرين مرة، فيما ارتفع عدد سكانها أكثر من عشرة اضعاف. واليوم، تشمخ أبو ظبي كواحدة من أهم المراكز الثقافية والاقتصادية في المنطقة.

يقدم هذا الكتاب وصفا وجيزا لتاريخ المدينة وتراثها وتطورها. والحقيقة ان عوامل عديدة تجمعت لتنتج هذه اللوحة البديعة المسماة أبو ظبي، وبينها تاريخ طويل من الاستيطان البشري الذي لم يتوقف، ومهارة السكان في الملاحة والتبادل التجاري مع المراكز التجارية الأخرى في الشرق الأوسط وجنوب آسيا. وفضلا عن ذلك، لعب سكان المنطقة دورا رئيسيا في بثِّ الدعوة الدينية وفي تزويد العالم بمفاهيم متجددة في الثقافة والعمارة والفنون. وقد أسهم كل ذلك في تطوير تراث أصيل يقف شامخا ليؤكد عراقة المنطقة وأصالة سكانها.

وتسعى هذه الطبعة الثانية من الكتاب الى تأكيد التزام الامارات العربية المتحدة وقادتها بربط الحاضر بالماضي كسبيل لصنع مستقبل مزدهر. والمأمول ان تثير هذه الطبعة المزيد من اهتمام القراء، القدماء منهم والجدد، عبر ما تقدمه لهم عن تاريخ وتراث وتطور مدينتنا الجميلة، أبو ظبي.

الشيخ نهيان بن مبارك آل نهيان
وزير التعليم العالي

ABU DHABI
GARDEN CITY OF THE GULF

by Peter Hellyer
and Ian Fairservice

MOTIVATE
PUBLISHING

**Published by
Motivate Publishing**

PO Box 2331, Dubai, UAE
Tel: 824060, Fax: 824436

PO Box 43072, Abu Dhabi, UAE
Tel: 311666, Fax: 311888

London House, 19 Old Court Place,
Kensington High Street, London W8 4PF
Tel: 0171 938 2222, Fax: 0171 937 7293

Directors: Obaid Humaid Al Tayer
& Ian Fairservice

First published 1988
First revised edition 1990
New edition 1992
Reprinted 1994
Fifth printing 1995

© 1992 Motivate Publishing

ISBN 1 873544 51 0

British Library Cataloguing-in-Publication
Data. A catalogue record for this book is
available from the British Library.

Printed by Emirates Printing Press, Dubai

CONTENTS

المحتويات

THE UNITED ARAB EMIRATES

The bright lights of the ever-changing skyline of Abu Dhabi city.

A quarter of a century ago, in March 1968, in response to an announcement by Britain that she was pulling out east of Suez in l971, the Rulers of seven sheikhdoms, known as the Trucial States, on the south-eastern flank of the Arabian Peninsula came together and agreed to establish a federation. They were disparate in size, ranging from small to tiny, and had a total population of only some 180,000. A few had no roads, no schools, no hospitals, no development at all, while conflict between them was a matter of recent memory, rather than distant history.

Yet, with changes ahead, after 150 years of a British presence, the seven Trucial States had no choice but to get together. Outside observers gave them little chance of success. As is so often the case, the observers have been proved wrong. In the years since the federation was established in 1971, the seven, joined as the United Arab Emirates, have undergone a rapid process of economic and social development within the protective shield of a political stability that has been able to weather not only the vicissitudes of regional conflicts, like Iraq's invasion of Kuwait, but also the impact of a population explosion, largely immigrant, that has seen the number of inhabitants rise more than ten-fold to over 1.8 million.

The citizens of the country, which comprises the Emirates of Abu Dhabi (by far the largest) Dubai, Sharjah, Ras Al Khaimah, Umm Al Quwain, Ajman and Fujairah, have seen their life style change utterly within a generation, after hundreds, perhaps thousands of years when their ancestors had struggled against the harsh natural environment.

The old ways involved survival, in the heat of summer, in one of the world's most severe deserts, or in the largely barren Hajar Mountains, with a scarcity of water occasionally relieved by rains, barely subsisting on pastoral nomadism or tiny mountain agricultural plots, or fighting the sea for its fish and pearls.

To survive, the people had to be tough and self-reliant, and life expectancy was low.

Today, thanks to the explosion of wealth from oil production, which began in 1962, even the smallest and poorest Emirates have advanced dramatically, and only in the remotest areas of the mountains can tribesmen still be found living in the old way — and that they do from choice rather than necessity. The rest enjoy all the benefits of a developed modern society.

منظر ليلي لكورنيش ابو ظبي بأبراجه المتلألئة وحدائقه البديعة.

Abu Dhabi

The Emirate of Abu Dhabi, which has provided the overwhelming bulk of the funds that have paid for the federation's development, is by far the largest of the seven, with an area of 80,000 square kilometres, 17 times larger than the second Emirate, Dubai, and amounting to over 86 per cent of the total area of the federation.

It has the largest population, 798,000 out of a total of 1.91 million, according to 1991 estimates, and has the bulk of the UAE's oil resources. Though

producing in late 1992 around two million barrels per day, it has the capacity to produce nearly half as much again, and has sufficient reserves for more than 150 years at present production rates, as well as the world's fourth largest reserves of natural gas.

Once a major power in south-eastern Arabia (see The Land, its Heritage and People) Abu Dhabi fell upon hard times in the 1930s and 1940s, partially due to the international economic depression and the Second World War that followed, and partially due to the Japanese invention of the cultured pearl, which destroyed the market for Abu Dhabi's most prized export — the pure, natural Gulf pearl.

Ironically, oil, the source of the economic miracle that has since changed the face of Abu Dhabi and the other Emirates, was also first produced from beneath the sea — or rather the sea-bed. The UAE's first producing field was at Umm Shaif, off Abu Dhabi, which was discovered in the late 1950s, and came on stream in 1962. A field found a little earlier on land, Bab, followed a year later, and Abu Dhabi entered the oil era. (See Oil and Gas: Fuel of Development).

In the 30 years that have passed, the Emirate of Abu Dhabi has been transformed, and has shared its good fortune with other members of the UAE. Fortunate to have as Ruler HH Sheikh Zayed bin Sultan Al Nahyan, who has been determined to put the oil revenues to good use ever since his accession in 1966, the Emirate has thrived.

If the main city, also called Abu Dhabi, has little today to recall the past, that's largely because until the oil-fuelled boom began, there really was very little of a town at all, let alone a city. Pictures less

than 30 years old show a scattering of barasti (palm-frond) huts or simple buildings made from coral, with a large white fort standing almost on its own, surrounded by a few palm trees.

Today that fort, appropriately the Government's Centre for Documentation and Research, is surrounded and dwarfed by high-rise buildings, for the city's skyline, best seen from off the imposing eight-kilometre-long Corniche, now resembles a mini-Manhattan.

Capital of the UAE as well as the Emirate, and also centre of the oil industry, Abu Dhabi may lack some of the commercial verve of its neighbour, Dubai, but it is, none the less, the wealthiest of all the UAE's cities. Laid out according to a simple grid plan first drafted 25 years ago, it is well-provided with parks, beaches and leisure centres which have made it the greenest city on the Gulf's coast — indeed, a pleasant place in which to live as well as to work.

The Emirate is, however, much more than just the city itself. Some 160 kilometres to the east lies

Three generations of a Bedouin family, photographed near Bu Hasa in the early 1970s.

عائلة بدوية من ثلاثة اجيال التقطت في صورة اوائل السبعينيات قرب بوحصا.

the inland city of Al Ain (See Al Ain: Oasis City) while to the west lie the great open spaces of the desert, reaching away south-west into the high rolling dunes of the Rub Al Khali, one of the most inhospitable places on earth.

This large area, the Emirate's Western Region, centred on the new desert township of Medinat Zayed, contains the onshore oilfields and the industrial complex of Ruwais — Jebel Dhanna on the coast, site of an oil export terminal, refinery and other installations.

It also contains the great arc of the Liwa Oasis, in reality a group of a couple of dozen little oases, the ancestral home of Abu Dhabi's ruling Al Nahyan family.

Weekend trips to the Liwa and camping in the desert have become popular pastimes for expatriate residents and tourists, following in the footsteps not only of the Bedouin of long ago, but also of today's Abu Dhabians, many of whom miss no opportunity to escape the hurly-burly and pressure of city life.

Though the gazelles after which the Emirate is named (Abu Dhabi means 'Father of the Gazelle') are now scarce and rarely seen, the real Abu Dhabi is to be found not in the splendid thoroughfares of the capital city, however impressive they may be, but in the wide open spaces where the gazelles and the Bedouin once roamed freely. If that sounds a little bit romantic — after all, life before oil was tough and the land unforgiving — a little bit of romance is still there to be found by any visitor.

Dubai

The second largest of the Emirates is Dubai. Occupying around 4,000 square kilometres of territory facing the Arabian Gulf, with a small mountain enclave at Hatta (now a popular holiday resort) Dubai has a trading history stretching back more than 2,000 years. It has an estimated population (1991 figures) of 501,000.

Ruled since 1990 by HH Sheikh Maktoum bin Rashid Al Maktoum, also the UAE's Vice-President and Prime Minister, Dubai has grown from a small

Hamdan Street, one of Abu Dhabi's main streets, and the commercial heart of the city.

شارع حمدان، قلب المدينة التجاري وأحد أهم شوارعها.

9

port astride a picturesque creek into the commercial centre of the region, and is now also becoming a popular tourist destination.

Blessed since the late 1960s with significant oil resources offshore, permitting production of around 400,000 barrels a day, and since the early 1980s with a major gas and condensate field onshore at Margham, Dubai has been well able to finance its own development. Of all the seven members of the UAE, it has most profited out of commerce and out of the wise creation of a diversified economic base decreed by Sheikh Rashid bin Saeed Al Maktoum, who ruled the Emirate from 1958 until his death in 1990. This now includes the Gulf's top aluminium plant DUBAL, a cable plant, and the largest man-made harbour in the world at Jebel Ali, around which an industrial and free trade zone is rapidly growing. Over one billion dollars have already been invested there.

Renowned throughout Arabia for its shopping, Dubai, the Gateway to the Gulf, is equally well-known in international business circles for the sophistication of its banking system, and for the facilities of its airport and ports. Dubai International Airport, home base of the rapidly growing Emirates airline, is used by over 50 airlines, while Port Rashid and Port Jebel Ali are amongst the region's busiest.

In 1992, the two handled well over a million containers.

As a commercial entrepot, Dubai is well-provided with luxury hotels. If until recently these were used mainly by businessmen, winter months now see them crowded with tourists from Europe and the United States, eager to sample traditional Arab hospitality, as well as the Emirate's other attractions — like camel and horse-racing, ice-skating and the finest golf courses in the Middle East.

Sharjah and the Northern Emirates

Stretching along the Arabian Gulf coast north of Dubai, and away across the Hajar Mountains to the Gulf of Oman on the other side are the UAE's remaining five Emirates.

The largest of these is Sharjah, with an area of around 2,600 square kilometres, and a population estimated at 314,000. Sharjah town, a mere 13 kilometres from Dubai, is the seat of the ruling Al Qasimi family (who also rule Ras Al Khaimah) descendants of the sheikhs who battled the British and whose fleets held sway over much of the Gulf and the Arabian Sea at the beginning of the 19th century.

That history is reflected in the fine old forts and

Dubai Creek, the focus of the city and a hive of trading activity with its flotilla of dhows.

خور دبي المزدحم بالمراكب هو محور المدينة وخلية نشاطها التجاري.

The Sharjah souk houses a traditional Arab bazaar inside a distinctive building.

بني سوق الشارقة على الطراز العربي التقليدي.

houses to be found in Sharjah itself, and in other coastal towns like Hamriyah. Thanks to its offshore Mubarak oilfield, adjacent to its offshore island of Abu Musa, and the much larger onshore gas and condensate field at Saja'a, Sharjah developed fast in the early 1980s. It now boasts a number of the country's most startling and innovative pieces of architecture, like the two souks (markets) both highly modern, but of Islamic-inspired design.

Home of the first modern school in the country, which opened less than 40 years ago, Sharjah also has a thriving intellectual and cultural tradition, with some of the UAE's finest writers and actors.

Adjacent is Ajman, surrounded by the Emirate of Sharjah and only 259 square kilometres in all, including the mountain enclaves of Masfut and Manama. Total population is around 76,000. The coastal town has little industry, apart from the Arab Heavy Engineering Shipyard. It has, however, a fine fort, used until recently as the Ruler's residence, and now a museum; while Ajman Creek is the best place in the UAE in which to see dhows being built by eye, not by blueprint, in the traditional manner.

Up the coast, past the Sharjah gas export terminal, is the next Emirate, Umm Al Quwain, perhaps the least developed of the seven. In recent years, it has benefited from the opening of a small free trade zone.

With the smallest population of all, an estimated 27,000 at the end of 1991, and an area of 780 square kilometres Umm Al Quwain has few resources, the offshore gas discovered in the 1970s yet to be declared commercial. Its fine old fort has been

beautifully restored as a museum, but the Emirate is now better known for the archaeological site of Ad Door, dating to between 200 BC and 200 AD, when it was the largest town in the lower Gulf, trading both with India and Rome.

Further up the coast comes Ras Al Khaimah, the other Al Qasimi Emirate, with a population of around 130,000 and an area of 1,700 square kilometres. It earns its living from a well-balanced mixture of agriculture, industry and limited oil production from the offshore Saleh oilfield, near the entrance to the Strait of Hormuz. Much of the area of Ras Al Khaimah is in the rugged and almost barren Hajar mountain range, where a few tribesmen still eke out a tough living amid conditions little changed for centuries.

The gravel plains between the mountains and the sea, however, are more fertile and Ras Al Khaimah has become one of the country's key producers of crops and livestock. The same plains must have been similarly fertile for thousands of years, for along the foot of the mountains hundreds of tombs have been found, dating back to the 3rd millennium BC.

In more recent, recorded history, Ras Al Khaimah figures prominently. Once known as Julfar, whose ruins are a few kilometres north of the modern town, it appears in the chronicles of the early Muslim caliphates, and traded with China. In the late 18th and early 19th century, the Al Qasimi rulers had the largest fleet in the Indian Ocean. A multi-national archaeological effort is now unlocking many of Julfar's secrets.

Over on the Gulf of Oman coast lies the seventh Emirate, Fujairah, with a 1991-estimated population of 63,000, and an area of 1,300 square kilometres. Connected in 1976 to the rest of the country by a tarmac road only, it has the most beautiful beaches in the UAE, of exquisitely fine sand, fringed by palm groves growing down almost to the water's edge, very different from the more sparsely vegetated Arabian Gulf coast.

Here, and in the rugged mountains behind, castles and forts, like that at Bithnah, recall a more troubled past that came to an end only recently. The old mud-brick castle at Fujairah, soon to be restored, has one tower built of breeze-block, used to repair a hole blasted in it by a British warship in the 1920s.

The coastline is shared with Sharjah, whose enclaves of Khor Fakkan and Kalba, and the shared town of Dibba, are equally attractive to the visitors who flock to the east coast at weekends from other Emirates. One popular sight is the little mosque at Bidiya, the oldest in the UAE. By a happy accident of geography, Fujairah and Khor Fakkan lie outside the Arabian Gulf, and their ports have thrived in recent years, now handling nearly one million containers a year.

This has helped to stimulate other aspects of commercial growth and, planning carefully, Fujairah has now built up a thriving commercial sector, with several small-scale industries in the town and around the port and airport to complement the income from tourism.

AL AIN
Oasis City

The oasis city of Al Ain looks both to the past and the future: to the past as the site of some of the oldest archaeological remains to be found in the country and to the future as the home of the Emirates University, the country's first seat of higher education.

Al Ain lies due east of Abu Dhabi in the lee of the great Hajar Mountains. Little more than 25 years ago it was a fairly ramshackle collection of six small villages, the largest called Al Ain, belonging to Abu Dhabi, situated next to three others, of which the largest is Buraimi, belonging to Oman. Each had its own falaj (underground irrigation channel) that brought water to the date groves and rudimentary agriculture on which people depended for their livelihood. The falaj system is at least 3,000 years old.

Today, seen from the air, it is a vast expanse of green, perhaps the largest in south-eastern Arabia, interspersed with modern roads, hospitals, housing, schools, old forts, the largest zoo in the Middle East, an ice-rink, a fun park, university campus, waving fields of wheat — all evidence of a judicious use of oil revenues making the desert bloom. Its airport opens in 1993.

The domes and minarets of the Hamdan bin Zayed Al Awal Mosque, Al Ain.

قبب ومآذن جامع حمدان بن زايد الاول في العين.

The Emirates University is the principal institute of higher education for young men and women of the UAE.

جامعة الامارات هي مؤسسة التعليم العليا الرئيسية لشبان الامارات من الجنسين.

A dream come true

The visionary behind it all is the Ruler of the Emirate and UAE President, HH Sheikh Zayed bin Sultan Al Nahyan. He spent much of his childhood in Al Ain, and was appointed Governor of the region in 1946, a post he held for 20 years before becoming Ruler in 1966. Over that period, he laid down the original plan for Al Ain's development which is now coming to maturity.

Al Ain, capital of Abu Dhabi's Eastern Region, is no longer a small village, but an impressive, well-planned city. Its population is now around 200,000 and rising, as the current Ruler's Representative Sheikh Tahnoun bin Mohammed Al Nahyan, puts into practice Sheikh Zayed's dreams.

Al Ain has managed to retain an atmosphere redolent of the essence of old Arabia, with its mud-brick forts (a number now well-restored and open to visitors), carefully cultivated palm groves, and the camel market that still attracts dealers from far and wide. It's not surprising that many local citizens whose jobs take them to Abu Dhabi rush home every weekend to Al Ain. Growing numbers of expatriates and tourists, too, regularly make the 320-kilometre round-trip from the capital to sample the attractions of the Oasis City.

One major attraction is its historical remains, from one of the first forts built locally by the Al Nahyan family around 175 years ago to prehistoric tombs more than 5,000 years old. The well-appointed museum, housed in a more recent fort, provides a good introduction to any aspiring amateur archaeologist or historian. (See The Land, its Heritage and People).

Antiquity, however, provides only one facet of Al Ain. The land itself can be quite stunning in its variety, from the whaleback mountain of Jebel Hafit, whose summit can be reached by a road, for those unwilling or unable to tackle the arduous climb, to the great dunes north and west of the city, or from the intricate channels and dams of a falaj-irrigated palm garden to the waving fields of wheat at Al Oha, or nearby cattle farms.

More evidence of man's involvement with nature can be found at the leisure park built around the natural spring at Ain Al Faidha and in the well-shaded acres of the zoo. Here hippopotami, elephants and lions gambol in the desert sun, and the world's largest herd of the fabled Arabian oryx

تجتذب حديقة الهيلي اعدادا كبيرة من الزوار ايام العطلات.

Hili Fun City's fairground attractions are a
magnet on public holidays.

مقبرة عمرها اكثر من ٥٠٠٠ سنة اكتشفت في منطقة الهيلي بالعين، واعيد تجديدها.

Hili Garden, featuring the reconstruction of a
tomb more than 5,000 years old, found at Al Ain.

can be seen, as well as several hundred other species of animals and birds; many acclimatised so well that they are breeding in abundance.

Both are popular points of call for residents and visitors alike. So, too, are two other of Al Ain's parks in the Hili district. One, the Hili Garden, is laid out around a reconstructed tomb more than 4,000 years old, and adjoins the now-excavated remains of a Bronze Age settlement. The other, Hili Fun City, has a more modern focus, a large fun fair attracting capacity crowds at weekends and on public holidays.

Industrial base

But Al Ain is not all leisure, even if its surroundings help to make it the most attractive of all inland Arabian cities. Adjoining Buraimi (whose falaj-fed palm gardens are a classic example of their type), and astride the main road route to the Gulf of Oman, it is an important point in overland trade, and is alone among the UAE's cities in being the focal point for a wide hinterland, which stretches deep into both desert and mountains. A thriving local commercial sector helps to support the demand for ever-improving health, education and housing facilities, that in turn stimulate the city's continued growth.

The Al Ain area is also the centre of the Emirate's

agriculture, producing more than 130,000 tons of crops a year worth over Dh175 million and with the nucleus of a profitable dairy farming industry. A canning factory and a cement plant increase its growing industrial base, while the opening of an international airport will add to the city's importance.

More and more, the main focus of attention in this inland oasis city is turning away from the past and the present to look towards the country's future, represented by the Zayed Military Academy (training young officers from all over the Gulf) and by the 10,000 or so students at the Emirates University. Founded in 1977, and now occupying a large and ever-growing campus on the city outskirts, it has already produced several thousand national graduates, men and women who are playing increasingly important roles as the Emirate and the UAE head towards the 21st century.

The Al Ain Men's College and Women's College, part of a national network of Higher Colleges of Technology, offer hundreds more students a more technically-oriented education.

Deeply anchored in its past, looking confidently to its future, Al Ain is a fascinating and crucial part of the Emirates today.

تضم حديقة حيوان العين مجموعة حيوانات نادرة مثل المها العربية.

Al Ain Zoo bouses a variety of indigenous animals, such as the Arabian Oryx.

Al Ain bas grown into an impressive, well-planned city.

تمتاز مدينة العين الحديثة بتخطيطها الجيد.

1

SHEIKH ZAYED

A man of his people

The President of the United Arab Emirates, HH Sheikh Zayed bin Sultan Al Nahyan, has led the seven-member federation since it was established in 1971, and has been Ruler of the largest Emirate, Abu Dhabi, since 1966. He has led both through a programme of change so rapid that it has few parallels, even in this era of Arabia's oil-fuelled development.

The pace has been so quick that it has been readily visible even to expatriates who have spent but a few years in the country; while photographs from 30 years ago show that, in the cities at least, Abu Dhabi and the UAE are virtually brand new. For Sheikh Zayed and his compatriots, it has been a veritable revolution.

The prospect of such wealth was too remote even to be a dream a little over 70 years ago, when the wife of Sheikh Sultan, a younger brother of the Ruler of Abu Dhabi, then one of the Trucial States, delivered her husband his fourth son. They named him Zayed, after his illustrious grandfather, Zayed bin Khalifa, who had ruled the Emirate from 1855-1909.

The event may have brought joy to the family, but it seemed unlikely that it would be of much other significance. The boy's father was only one of a number of brothers; Abu Dhabi was poor and off the beaten track of international diplomacy; and certainly the British Political Agent in the region made little mention in his reports of the birth.

Half a century later the boy was to step into his grandfather's shoes to begin a reign that has brought his country regional and international prominence, 13th in a line of rulers that stretches back nearly 250 years.

Any assessment of his achievements, of course — and there are many — must be set in the context of the world into which the young Zayed was born, and in which he grew to manhood.

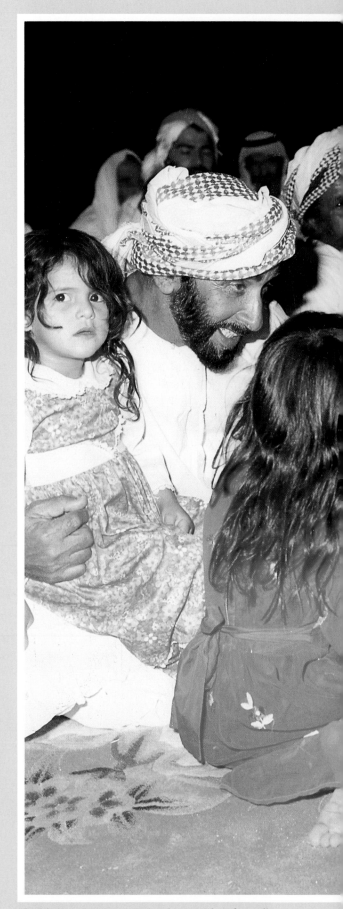

Sheikh Zayed enjoys meeting his people informally, talking with them and playing with their children.

16

١

زايد..
قائد
المسيرة

كان يوم ٦ أغسطس ١٩٦٦ نقطة تحول رئيسية في تاريخ البلاد لأنه اليوم الذي تسلم فيه صاحب السمو الشيخ زايد بن سلطان آل نهيان رئيس دولة الامارات العربية المتحدة وحاكم أبوظبي مقاليد الحكم في الامارة... واليوم الذي بدأت فيه حركة البناء والتقدم التي وضعت الدولة في طريقه التطور والازدهار.

وخلال تلك السنوات كرس صاحب السمو الشيخ زايد كل جهده لاعلاء شأن البلاد وتوفير الحياة الكريمة لابنائها.

ويتجلى ذلك واضحاً في حرص سموه على تفقد أحوال المواطنين في المدن والمناطق النائية على حد سواء ومتابعة سير العمل في المشاريع التنموية والتوجيه باقامة المزيد منها في مختلف أنحاء البلاد.وكان له الدور الرئيسي في قيام دولة الامارات العربية المتحدة.

ولم تقتصر انجازات صاحب السمو الشيخ زايد على الصعيد المحلي فقط، اذ كان له دور رئيسي في قيام مجلس التعاون لدول الخليج العربية، وتحت قيادة سموه لعبت الامارات دوراً سياسياً بارزاً على الصعيدين العربي والعالمي.

واستطاع صاحب السمو رئيس الدولة بفضل ايمانه الراسخ بمستقبل الوطن وقدرات شعبه أن ينتقل به خلال فترة قصيرة الى مصاف الدول المتقدمة، واضعاً مصلحة الوطن فوق أي اعتبار. وتحت قيادة سموه قطعت دولة الامارات العربية المتحدة شوطاً كبيراً في مجال التقدم الاقتصادي والصناعي والزراعي والنفطي والعمراني والاجتماعي وتغيرت ملامح الطبيعة على هذه الأرض الخيرة في اتجاه التطوير والتحديث المستمر، لتصبح واحدة من أسرع الدول تطوراً ونمواً في العالم.

يحرص صاحب السمو الشيخ زايد بن سلطان آل نهيان رئيس الدولة على لقاء المواطنين وقضاء بعض الوقت مع اطفالهم.

صاحب السمو الشيخ زايد يحمل واحدا من صقوره. وقد شبَّ سموه في مدينة العين والصحراء المجاورة، حيث تعلم رياضة الصيد بالصقور التي ما زال يمارسها حتى الآن.

Sheikh Zayed, pictured with one of his falcons. In his youth, he spent much time in Al Ain and the surrounding desert learning to shoot and to hunt with falcons, a sport he still practises.

The backwardness that characterised the area in the 1920s and 1930s limited his opportunities for education to simple instruction in a Quranic school. Despite this, however, he developed the convictions, the principles, and the skills that would later help him as a leader.

His father, Sultan, ruled the Emirate from 1922 until his death in 1926, and, following a short reign by an uncle, little more than a year later, in early 1928, Zayed's eldest brother Shakhbut was chosen as Ruler, inaugurating a period of political stability.

Sheikh Zayed grew to manhood in the years that followed, spending much of his time in Al Ain and in the surrounding desert, learning to shoot and to hunt with falcons, the latter a sport he practises still; and also learning the ways of the tribes that peopled Abu Dhabi and its neighbouring Emirates.

Riding his camel far across the desert, he saw at first hand the age-old tribal conflicts, and the effect they had upon the land and the people. He watched, too, as wiser heads sought to mediate and to conciliate, learning that, in a harsh environment, the struggle for survival may be the most important challenge of all. He absorbed knowledge of his people's culture and traditions, and came, too, as had the Bedouin for over 1,000 years before him, to develop a deep belief in the religion of Islam. They remain essential parts of his character and beliefs today.

The desert felt little of the turmoil affecting the rest of the world in the 1930s though the collapse of the market for Gulf pearls reduced the Emirate to near-bankruptcy. One faint hint of the future to come, however, did make its way across the sands: an early geological prospecting team, carrying out a survey for traces of oil. Sheikh Zayed, little more than 20, was assigned the task of guiding them on their path.

By 1946 Zayed had won a reputation, not only

سمو الشيخ خليفة بن زايد آل نهيان ولي عهد ابو ظبي ونائب القائد
الاعلى للقوات المسلحة.

Sheikh Khalifa bin Zayed Al Nahyan, Crown Prince of Abu Dhabi and Deputy Supreme Commander of the Armed Forces.

in Abu Dhabi, but also in neighbouring Oman, of being an influential tribal leader, despite his relative youth. As the great explorer of inner Arabia, Wilfred Thesiger, noted in his book *Arabian Sands*, the Bedouin admired him greatly.

"They liked him for his easy informal ways and his friendliness, and they respected his force of character, his shrewdness, and his strength."

In that year, his brother appointed him Ruler's Representative in Al Ain. For the next 20 years, learning as he went, Sheikh Zayed was to prove that the expression of confidence was by no means misplaced.

They were not easy years. Sheikh Zayed was keen to bring development to Al Ain, but money was scarce. Cajoling his relatives to give up their rights to the limited water resources, he cleaned out the ancient falaj system so that more water became available. Agriculture thrived, and so did Al Ain.

Establishing a school in the late 1950s, he was again hampered by a lack of funds. He responded by paying the teachers from his own pocket — and among the children benefiting were some of the country's prominent figures today, like Abu Dhabi Crown Prince and Armed Forces Deputy Supreme Commander, Sheikh Khalifa bin Zayed, Deputy Prime Minister and Public Works Department Chairman Sheikh Sultan bin Zayed, the current Ruler's Representative in Al Ain Sheikh Tahnoun, and Presidential Court Chamberlain, Sheikh Surour.

Problems within were joined by problems from without. The end of the Second World War brought new interest in the region's oil resources. Company rivalries were paralleled by territorial claims, and for several years Sheikh Zayed was obliged to face a confrontation with Saudi Arabia over ownership of some Omani villages near Al Ain, and also over part of the Emirate.

With his active involvement, the status quo was re-established in 1955, and nearly 20 years later, Sheikh Zayed, as UAE President, and King Faisal of Saudi Arabia signed an agreement to bring the dispute to an end.

The arrival of oil in the Emirate was not long delayed. The first well was drilled in 1950, and the first commercial field, Bab, was discovered in 1958. Production began in 1962. The new revenues meant that the pressure for progress grew. Sheikh Zayed was an obvious choice as a new Ruler to guide Abu Dhabi into uncharted waters.

In a book published in 1964, British author Clarence Mann said of him: "Sheikh Zayed is the principal authority in Buraimi (Al Ain), and from here his influence stretches throughout Dhafra. He is highly respected by the Bedouins, because he knows and practises their ways and traditions. It is through him that Abu Dhabi exerts its influence on the Bedouins and this factor, plus his reputation for justice, advancement and statesmanship would almost ensure that he would be chosen as his brother's successor."

So it was. When Sheikh Shakhbut abdicated on 6th August, 1966, Sheikh Zayed took on the task.

In the early years, he was a man in a hurry. Those that worked with him recall the frenetic activity as orders flowed to get the Emirate on the move. Within days, a formal Government structure had been established, with departments to tackle the individual functions. Instructions were given for housing, schools, health services, a port, an airport, roads, a bridge to link Abu Dhabi to the mainland, and so on.

For the Bedouin, a programme of well-drilling was instituted, to ease the search for water while the recently founded Abu Dhabi Defence Force realised that one task of its mobile patrols was to bring basic medical skills to remote areas.

Typically, Sheikh Zayed, who had grown to love Al Ain deeply, didn't forget his dreams to develop the town. Money was poured into the planting of trees that have today made Al Ain the Oasis City of the Gulf and, in what seemed an amazing move at the time, Sheikh Zayed set aside a plot of desert near Jebel Hafit in 1967, and hired an Austrian animal lover to found a zoo. Twenty years later, it's the most impressive in the region.

If Sheikh Zayed was impatient for progress for his people, he did not forget the commitment to cooperation with his neighbours forged in his youth.

One early step was to meet with the then Ruler of Dubai, Sheikh Rashid bin Saeed Al Maktoum — later the first UAE Vice-President and Prime Minister — to resolve a long-standing border dispute. Other agreements were signed with Oman and Qatar. He also pumped funds into the Trucial States Development Council, showing his willingness to share Abu Dhabi's good fortune with others.

When, in early 1968, the British announced their intention of leaving the Gulf, it was natural that Sheikh Zayed and Sheikh Rashid took the lead in calling for a federation of the Gulf Emirates that finally emerged as the UAE nearly four years later.

The status of Abu Dhabi and the UAE today is largely the result of efforts made by Sheikh Zayed, as Ruler and as President; the state is a record of his work, much of which can be seen elsewhere in this book. Inside the country and outside, the influence of his beliefs can be traced in that record.

The belief in cooperation rather than confrontation can be seen in his building of the federation, and in the leading role the UAE plays in the Gulf Cooperation Council and in bodies like the Arab League and the Islamic Conference Organisation. The skills in conciliation have been put to work in a regional and wider framework, while pride in his Arab heritage has led to Sheikh Zayed's determined commitment to the Palestinian cause.

Abroad and at home, the President's deeply held faith has continued to guide him. "It is Islam that asks every Muslim to respect every person," he believes. "Not, I emphasise, special people, but every person. In short, to treat every person, no matter what his creed or race, as a special soul is a mark of Islam. It is just such a point embodied in Islam's tenets, that makes us proud of Islam. To be together, to trust each other as human beings, to behave as equals."

If that has inspired his belief in the necessity of sharing Abu Dhabi's wealth with others less fortunate — it has, too, underpinned his ability to resist the seductive lure of pomp and circumstance. Perhaps that is why it is so uncommon to hear criticisms of Sheikh Zayed. Of the country's administration, maybe, even of ministers, but it is rare indeed to hear them of the President. After more than 25 years as Ruler and more than 20 years as President, whether he is travelling as a head of state, dancing at a wedding, visiting a school or watching a camel race, UAE residents, expatriates and citizens alike, know well that Sheikh Zayed remains not a man for, but a man of, his people.

بتوجيه من صاحب السمو الشيخ زايد، تنتشر في ابو ظبي المرافق العصرية جنبا الى جنب مع المساجد الحديثة.

Traditional Islamic faith and modern technology exist side by side in the development of Abu Dhabi during Sheikh Zayed's rule.

2

THE LAND, ITS HERITAGE AND PEOPLE

Forty years ago, Wilfred Thesiger, the last of the great European explorers of the Arabian Peninsula, made his classic journey by camel from southern Oman across the wastes of the Rub Al Khali, the Empty Quarter, to the shores of the Arabian Gulf.

The story, told in his book *Arabian Sands*, is one of intense hardship as he and his Bedouin companions struggled through the trackless, waterless deserts and across the high rolling dunes, urging their camels onwards to the water-holes and oases and to the Gulf beyond. It is a story, too, of man's ability to survive in a land where nature itself seems determined to resist his presence.

Part of that journey lay within the Emirate of Abu Dhabi, and Thesiger's descriptions of his arrival in the Liwa Oasis and of his happy interlude hunting with the current Ruler and UAE President, Sheikh Zayed, in the hinterland of Al Ain are not only masterpieces of travel writing, but are also the best available descriptions in the English language of a way of life now vanished and but a fading memory. *Arabian Sands* was published in Arabic for the first time in 1990, by Motivate Publishing.

Unlike the other six Emirates that together make up the UAE, Abu Dhabi is largely desert, with the dunes imperceptibly but relentlessly moving, year by year, across the land. For countless generations before Thesiger's arrival, the Bedouin of the area had lived and survived — even if they hadn't thrived — in the harsh desert conditions. If today the flow of oil revenues has brought prosperity and development, it is a recent change.

The 80,000 square kilometres of the Emirate of Abu Dhabi lie on the south-eastern flank of the Arabian Peninsula, adjoining the southern shores of the Arabian Gulf. Bounded by Qatar

منظر بديع لمركب خشبي شراعي. وفي الصورة داخل الاطار بدوي معمر لوحت شمس الصحراء وجهه.

In full sail, a dhow makes an impressive sight. Inset: Sun and sand have etched the face of an old desert dweller.

٢ الارض والتراث

تقع أبوظبي جنوب شرقي شبه الجزيرة العربية على السواحل الجنوبية للخليج العربي، ولها حدود مشتركة مع قطر والسعودية في الشمال والشمال الغربي وسلطنة عمان في الجنوب والشرق ودبي والشارقة في الشمال الشرقي.

وتتراوح تضاريس الامارة التي تبلغ مساحتها ٨٠ الف كيلومتر مربع بين المناطق الساحلية المنبسطة والجزر المختلفة الاحجام والصحراء المترامية الاطراف والواحات الخضراء.

وقد ورد اسم أبوظبي لاول مرة في القرن السابع عشر عندما تولت عائلة آل نهيان الحكم في ليوا وهناك قصة وراء تسميتها بهذا الاسم، حيث روي ان الشيخ دياب بن عيسى ارسل عددا من الرجال في رحلة صيد، وعندما عادوا اخبروه بمشاهدتهم ظبيا في جزيرة قبالة الساحل فسماها أبوظبي وأمر بانشاء قرية فيها لموقعها الاستراتيجي وسرعان ما نمت هذه القرية وتوسعت حتى اصبحت عاصمة للامارة في عام ١٧٩٣.

وكان صيد السمك والغوص بحثا عن اللؤلؤ والتجارة والزراعة أهم الانشطة الاقتصادية لسكان الامارة منذ قرون

واكتشفت في مناطق مختلفة من الامارة حفريات اثرية يعود تاريخ بعضها الى ٤ الاف سنة مضت، موفرة بذلك شواهد حية على التاريخ العريق للمنطقة.

ورغم التطور الحضاري والاجتماعي والاقتصادي الكبير الذي شهدته ابوظبي خلال العقدين الماضيين الا ان الامارة حافظت على تراثها العريق فمازال الصيد بالصقور وسباق الهجن العربية الاصيلة واحتفالات الرقص الشعبي وسباقات القوارب الخشبية تقام بين حين وآخر تطبيقا لشعار «من لا ماضي له لا مستقبل له».

and Saudi Arabia in the west and south-west, by Oman in the south and east, and by the Emirates of Dubai and Sharjah in the north-east, it is made up mainly of arid gravel plains and sandy deserts, with large areas of sabhka (salt flats) along the coast. Offshore are several dozen islands, some large, like Abu Al Abyad, others little more than coral outcrops; while in the east, in the Al Ain area, the Emirate's border runs in the lee of the Hajar mountain range.

If the predominant feature is desert, there are oases amid the sand, the best known of which are the large oasis of Al Ain, in the east (see Al Ain: Oasis City) and the arc of small oases known as the Liwa in the south, the last secure source

of water before the mountainous dunes of the Rub Al Khali.

Al Ain and the Liwa have traditionally been two of the three geographic pillars on which the Emirate stands, the third being the island of Abu Dhabi, capital both of the Emirate and of the UAE.

The Emirate first appears in history during the 17th century, when the Al Nahyan family emerged as the rulers of the Liwa-based Bani Yas tribal confederation, a Bedouin alliance that traced its origins back to the far west of Arabia.

The Bani Yas shared the Liwa with the Manasir, (Mansouris), another tribe still prominent today, and it was from the Liwa, or so the story goes, that Sheikh Dhiyab bin Isa sent out a hunting party

Left: The historic watchtower overlooks the Al Maqta'a Bridge leading to Abu Dhabi Island. Below: A shady corner in the courtyard of Abu Dhabi's old fort.

in 1761 that was to change the history of southern Arabia.

According to tribal tradition, the hunting party followed the track of a gazelle near the coast, and then across a narrow inlet at low tide. When the coastal mist lifted, they saw the gazelle drinking at a spring of brackish water. What happened to the gazelle is not related, but when the party returned to the Liwa to tell Sheikh Dhiyab of their discovery, he decreed that the island should be known as Abu Dhabi (The 'Father' or homeland of the Gazelle).

Recognising the importance of Abu Dhabi's water, a rare occurrence along the Gulf coastline, Sheikh Dhiyab ordered a village to be established on the island. Although he chose to remain in Liwa, his son and successor, Sheikh Shakhbut bin Dhiyab moved there in 1793, since when Abu Dhabi has been the Emirate's capital. He built a small fort around the spring. Much extended, that fort is today the Al Hisn Palace, home of the Centre for Documentation and Research.

The third pillar of the growing Emirate was Al Ain, traditional home of the powerful Dhawahir (Dhahiri) tribe, with whom Sheikh Shakhbut made an alliance early in the 19th century, building a fort in 1818 whose crumbling remains still survive. To complete the interlocking tribal alliances that made up the Emirate's population, the Bani Yas also established ties with the nomadic Awamir (Amiri) who roamed over the desert to the south and west of Liwa.

The four tribes and the three centres of population provided the foundations of the Emirate. The Al Ain oasis, with its lush palm groves and ample supplies of subterranean water flowing through underground channels, or falajes, some as much as 3,000 years old, provided a simple agricultural base, supplemented by the smaller and poorer palms in Liwa and the sparse desert rangeland nearby.

The other main source of income was from the waters of the Gulf. The best pearl oyster beds in the Gulf stretch across the great bay extending eastwards from the Qatar Peninsula, and have been yielding up their pearls for thousands of years. Excavations on local sites more than 4,500 years

old have shown that the area's ancient inhabitants knew and prized pearls.

Traditionally, any local boat-owner has been able to search for pearls on the oyster beds, regardless of his place of origin. Once Sheikh Shakhbut bin Dhiyab had moved his headquarters to Abu Dhabi island from the Liwa, however, then oyster beds all fell within Abu Dhabi's waters, giving the growing Emirate additional economic importance. While traders and pearl-divers from other areas could continue to operate, they were permitted to do so only if they paid taxes to the Ruler.

His own people were also able to profit from the pearling. A pattern of seasonal migration had long existed, to allow the best use to be made of the scanty resources both onshore and offshore. The Bani Yas was a confederation of sub-tribes (all accepting the leadership of the Al Nahyan family) including such names as the Suweidis, the Mazrouis, the Muheirbis, the Hamilis, the Qubeisis and the Rumaithis.

Among some groups, the Hamili and Qubeisi tribes in particular, the winter months were spent in the Liwa or in the desert, while the men went offshore to the pearling grounds during the summer.

The control of the pearl grounds gave Abu Dhabi an incentive to ensure that peace was maintained in the area, for any fighting would disrupt the pearl harvest. When, in the period after the arrival of the British in 1820, the imperial power sought to persuade the Emirates along the coast to agree to an annual truce at sea during the pearling season, Abu Dhabi accepted with alacrity. The Treaty of Maritime Truce eventually became permanent — and gave to the area the name by which it was known until independence in 1971, the Trucial States.

From 1855 until 1909, the reign of Sheikh Zayed bin Khalifa (Zayed the First), a grandson of Sheikh Shakhbut bin Dhiyab, saw Abu Dhabi rise to become a power throughout south-eastern Arabia,

Pearl divers went through their catch every day with the captain of the pearling boat.

فتح المحار بحثا عن اللؤلؤ بعد قيام الغواصين باصطياده.

عملية بناء مركب تقليدي تقارب نهايتها في حوض بناء المراكب.
يحتاج تثبيت الدعائم العرضية لمهارة كبيرة (ادناه).

A traditional Gulf dhow takes shape in the builder's yard.
Below: An adze is used to fit the boat's ribs.

with influence stretching deep into inner Oman and the desert wastes of the Rub Al Khali, and up into what now comprises the Northern Emirates.

Though in subsequent years, the size of the Emirate declined, it retained much of its importance and with the oil wealth beginning to flow in the 1960s, naturally took a prominent role in the formation of the United Arab Emirates under the present Ruler, Sheikh Zayed bin Sultan, a grandson of Zayed the First.

Relics of an ancient past

If the Emirate of Abu Dhabi, as such dates back only two or three hundred years, the history of the area now comprising the Emirate stretches much further back, and in recent years, archaeological excavations by both foreign and local teams have shown that it played a prominent role in the development of civilisation in this corner of Arabia.

Isolated finds of flint implements in the desert can be dated back to at least around 6,000 BC, perhaps as much as 200,000 BC, but the first hard evidence of permanent settlement is later dating to the early 4th millennium BC (around 3,200 BC). Since that time, at least, it seems, the Emirate has been permanently inhabited.

The story of the discovery of the first relics of Abu Dhabi's past to be uncovered in modern times is itself suitable for a detective novel. During the 1950s, a Danish team was excavating in Bahrain when the members were informed by a British amateur archaeologist working for one of Abu Dhabi's oil companies that there seemed to be burial mounds on the tiny island of Umm Al Nar, adjacent to Abu Dhabi island.

27

يضم متحف العين ثروة من القطع الفنية التي عثرت عليها بعثات
التنقيب عن الآثار منذ الخمسينيات، مثل هذه الجرة التي تعود للألف
الثاني قبل الميلاد.
جدران مستوطنة من العصر الحديدي في العين (ادناه).

Above: Al Ain Museum displays a wealth of artifacts from archaeological expeditions mounted since the 1950s, such as this second millennium chlorite jar.
Below: Walls of an Iron Age settlement in Al Ain.

When they came down to look, they found round tombs and a settlement dating back to the middle of the 3rd millennium BC, from a culture hitherto unknown, and now named the Umm Al Nar culture. The site produced the first evidence known anywhere of the domestication of the camel, that familiar ship of the Arabian desert, and also yielded finds that proved the people of Umm Al Nar, over 4,000 years ago, were trading with Mesopotamia and the Indian subcontinent.

Hearing of the Danish team at work, Sheikh Zayed, then the Ruler's representative in Al Ain, came to look at their finds. They should, he told them, come up to Al Ain as well, for on the foothills and the crest of nearby Jebel Hafit there were also piles of stones that might be worth examining.

Accepting Sheikh Zayed's invitation, the Danes travelled to Al Ain, to find literally hundreds of tombs on the top of Jebel Hafit, and on the tops of other mountains nearby, dating back, excavation proved, to the early 4th millennium BC.

Such was the beginning of archaeology in Abu Dhabi — and since then, with the active encouragement of Sheikh Zayed, scarcely a year has

passed without an excavation somewhere in the Emirate yielding new information about the area's past. Small sites have been found at various points along the coast, like Ras Al Aysh and Khor Ghanadah, but the most extensive and most exciting discoveries have been made throughout the Al Ain oasis.

An oasis for at least 5,000 years, its supplies of fresh water were as attractive to early inhabitants as they were in the recent past. Most interesting to the visitor is the complex of sites in the Hili area, which includes a number of settlements, a falaj dating back to around 1,000 BC, and the now-famous Hili Tomb, a round stone structure with bas-relief carvings of men and animals that has been carefully re-constructed. It now stands in the middle of one of Al Ain's lush public gardens, and, like many of the other local sites, can be freely visited. Offshore, on some of Abu Dhabi's many islands, there have recently been other major discoveries, including Stone Age flint 'factories', and a 6,000-year-old trading village.

The best of the finds from Hili and from other sites in the Emirate are on display in the Al Ain Museum, housed next to a carefully-modernised fort not far from the camel market.

القراقير هي احد اهم وسائل صيد الاسماك في المنطقة منذ القديم. وتصنع من اسلاك معدنية رفيعة.

Fish, staple food of Gulf people, were caught in traps such as this which formerly were woven of date frond strips.

Symbol of Arab hospitality: Abu Dhabi's Coffee Pot Fountain at sunset.

منظر دلّـة القهوة رمز الضيافة العربية عند الغروب.

Traditional sports and entertainment are very much in evidence, from falconry, racing in rowing boats or on the backs of camels and horses, to music played on goatskin bagpipes, Oriental flute and drums, and dancing on festive occasions such as Eid or a sheikh's wedding.

The people and their heritage

One popular part of the museum's collection is an ethnographic display showing how the inhabitants of the Emirate lived in the days before oil — the Bedouin tents, the simple farming implements, the camel saddles and old rifles, all are on display. So too are examples of local jewellery, and other items of everyday use, some of which can still be bought by the discerning buyer from antique shops in both Al Ain and Abu Dhabi.

The display provides the visitor with a brief introduction to the heritage of the people of Abu Dhabi, which, though lacking great written literature or imposing non-military architecture, is none the less of considerable interest.

Deriving their livelihood both from the land and the sea, the people of Abu Dhabi had a culture before oil that reflected the influences of both, in their sports, in their poetry, in their way of life.

While the oral poetry, naturally, cannot be rendered easily into English, there is poetry enough in the physical aspects of the culture. The great days of the sailing dhows trading with India and East Africa, or of the pearling dhows that went out to harvest the Gulf's oysters, have now gone, but

the tradition of sailing lives on. Several times a year, the Government, keen to foster an interest in the national heritage, sponsors races for sailing dhows just off the Abu Dhabi Corniche, and the sight of a dozen triangular sails racing against the wind as similar sails have done for centuries has a poetry of its own for all but the most hard-hearted.

Another local maritime sport, to be seen at the same time as the dhow races, is the racing of rowing boats. No coxed fours or eights these — each boat may have up to 200 oarsmen, chanting ageless rhythmic seamen's songs as they pull their blades through the water.

Onshore, three sports retain popularity. The most familiar to the outsider is horse-racing, both with the thoroughbreds of Europe and North America, and with horses of Arab lineage, descended from the ancestors of the great European racing lines. Though unsuited for the desert, the horse has always been popular in Arabia. Many prominent Abu Dhabians still maintain stables, while occasional races are held during the winter months, under the aegis of the UAE Equestrian Federation.

Perhaps the most typical of local sports is falconry, still practised today by the highest and the most humble in the land, with saker or peregrine falcons

لا يزال التراث العريق حيًا في المناسبات الاجتماعية والرياضات التقليدية، المتمثلة بالصيد بالصقور، وسباقات قوارب التجديف وسباقات الهجن والخيول، وموسيقى القرب والطبول التي تمارس في الاعياد والاحتفالات.

bought or captured, and then trained to answer to their master's voice. From October to March, falcons can be seen on their owners' arms throughout the Emirate, in the car, at home, even in the bank or the shops, but, above all, being trained out on the sands as the Bedouin of Arabia have trained falcons for hundreds of years. The hunting of the quarry, usually the Houbara Bustard or the Stone Curlew, now generally takes place abroad, as the whole of the Emirate has been declared a conservation area by Sheikh Zayed, keen to preserve local wildlife.

Today, the hunting is carried out from Range Rovers or Toyota Land Cruisers, but until the coming of oil, the falconers rode out on their camels, hawks on their wrists. No longer the preferred mode of transport, the camel remains, however, an integral part of local life. In the cities, and in the villages, the local people still keep camels for their milk, and the number of beasts in the Emirate continues to grow year by year, encouraged by Government subsidies for camel-owners.

سيدة بدوية تصنع نسيجا مطرزا محليا يسمي التلي

A Bedouin woman making a kind of Arabic lace called telli.

Young jockeys rein in their camels as trainers make their last-minute adjustments to equipment.

The main role of the camel in Abu Dhabi in the 1990s however, is not as a source of milk, or as a means of transport, but as a sporting animal. Every winter, from October to April, camel races are held at tracks throughout the Emirates almost every weekend, culminating with the great annual races in April at Al Wathba, 40 kilometres east of Abu Dhabi, which attract top racers from all over the Arabian Peninsula. With prizes totalling millions of dirhams at stake, it's not surprising that the top camels themselves are worth a pretty sum. One highly-fancied Omani racing camel changed hands in 1987 for Dh15 million. Prices of Dh5 million or Dh6 million are almost commonplace.

The races themselves provide an opportunity to see local society at its most informal and democratic; simple tribesmen from the desert rubbing shoulders with sheikhs in a common fascination with the sport. The expatriate visitor is always welcome — as traditional Arab hospitality demands — but is always an outsider, a guest — a rare feature in Abu Dhabi today, where imported skills, technology and customs prevail in so many aspects of life.

Arab hospitality remains a key to the understanding of the people of Abu Dhabi, and of their country. Forged in the harsh struggle that was life before the coming of oil, the hospitality of the Bedouin became a code of conduct so deep-rooted that a traveller coming across a desert encampment could be sure of food and shelter, from what little was available, even if on occasion his hosts were, at the same time, his tribal enemies.

A philosophy of sharing is, of course, part of the religion of Islam, which took a hold in the Emirates during the lifetime of the Prophet Mohammed (peace be upon him) and is today a sturdy support to which the people of Abu Dhabi can hold fast amid the rapid changes that have swept away so much of their previous way of life. It helps to provide, perhaps, a guarantee that, however fast and far-reaching the changes, the essential nature of the culture and heritage of the people will remain.

المتسابقون يتلقون التعليمات الاخيرة من مضمري الهجن قبل انطلاق السباق.

3

COMMERCE AND INDUSTRY

The early 1990s have been a period both of challenges and of progress for the Emirate of Abu Dhabi, and for the United Arab Emirates as a whole. The August 1990 Iraqi invasion of Kuwait, and the subsequent successful expulsion of the Iraqi forces by an international coalition, including the UAE, in early 1991, was perhaps the greatest challenge faced by the Emirates since the oil era began in 1962. The 1979-1988 conflict between Iraq and Iran caused concern, but little in the way of fears for the UAE's own economy, which continued to grow throughout most of the period, apart from fluctuating expenditure caused by changes in oil revenues.

The Kuwait crisis, however, threatened the stability of the entire region, and also meant that massive new military expenditure was required. Abu Dhabi, like other states in the Emirates, has justly prided itself over the past 20 years for its communal harmony, and for its free-wheeling free enterprise system. Because of its social stability, for citizens and expatriates alike, it had managed by the end of the 1980s to have weathered regional storms, with its population and economy continuing to grow at a steady rate.

The Kuwait invasion threatened all that. Expatriates of several communities considered flight, while there was, naturally, a substantial outflow of capital as the more nervous transferred their funds overseas.

When the crisis began, the UAE Central Bank, headquartered in Abu Dhabi, took the decision to permit capital transfers to continue unchecked, supplying funds, as required, in both US dollars and UAE dirhams, to those locally-registered banks that required them.

As the Central Bank noted in its 1991 Annual Report, this wise policy "contributed to restoring

Modern towers along Abu Dhabi's Corniche mirror the country's commercial development.

يعد النفط بمثابة العمود الفقري لاقتصاد امارة أبوظبي فحتى قبل سنوات كان يشكل الجزء الاعظم من الناتج المحلي، الا انه الحكومة وحرصا ً منها على بناء اقتصاء متين وتحقيق معدلات نمو مستقرة ومتوازنة ولتجنب اثار التقلبات الحادة في اسعار وعائدات النفط عنى الاقتصاد المحلي فقد عملت على تشجيع وتنمية مختلف القطاعات الاخرى وخاصة الصناعة والزراعة والتجارة.

وساعد وجود بنية اساسية متكاملة مثل المواني البحرية والجوية الحديثة وشبكة الطرق وامدادات الوقود والكهرباء والماء على تحقيق معدلات صناعية وزراعية وتجارية تعد الاعلى من نوعها في العالم.

وفي المجال الصناعي نالت الصناعة النفطية قدرا ً كبيرا ً من الاهتمام فاقيمت المصافي النفطية ومصانع البتروكيماويات كما نشط القطاع الخاص في اقامة العديد من المصانع وتشير الاحصائيات الى ان عدد المنشآت الصناعية فى الامارة بلغ العام الماضي ٢١٢٦ منشاة

وشهد القطاع التجاري ايضا معدلات نمو قياسية مع تزايد اهمية الامارة كمركز تجاري دولي وقفز حجم مبادلاتها التجاري مع العالم الى ٧٫٥ مليار درهم العام الماضي وسجلت اعادة الصادرات ارتفاعا ً كبيرا ً على مدى الاعوام الثلاث الماضية وخاصة الى دول مجلس التعاون الخليجي.

وفي المجال الزراعي تضاعف انتاج الامارة من الخضار والفواكه عدة مرات بفضل الدعم والتشجيع الحكومي للمزارعين، اذ ارتفع انتاج الخضار عام ٨٦ مثلا الى ٧٥٠٠٠ طن قيمتها ٩٠ مليون درهم وذلك مقابل ٣٢ الف طن عام ١٩٨٢.

تعكس الابراج المنتشرة على كورنيش ابو ظبي تطورها التجاري.

يطل برج غرفة تجارة وصناعة ابو ظبي على دوار الساعة.

The Chamber of Commerce Tower overlooks the Clock Tower Roundabout.

continued rise of the non-oil sector, both in real terms, and as a percentage of the overall Gross Domestic Product, GDP.

Abu Dhabi has sufficient oil reserves to continue production at current rates of around two million barrels a day for well over a century, while it has, at the same time, the fourth largest reserves of natural gas in the world.

Despite this, however, it has been Government policy for many years to encourage the diversification of the economy, into industry and agriculture, shipping and tourism, finance and construction, so that economic health is less subject to the fluctuations of prices and demand of the international oil market.

The sharp decline of oil prices in the early 1980s halved Government revenues, underlining the value of diversification and the last few years have seen the non-oil sector of GDP overtake and clearly outstrip the contributions of the oil sector.

ln 1990, nearly half of which was affected by the Kuwait crisis, GDP continued to grow — up by 23.2 per cent from Dh101.8 billion in 1989 to Dh125.4 billion, made up of an increase in the value-added of the oil sector by 48.7 per cent, thanks to greater oil prices, and of non-oil sectors by 7.5 per cent.

Despite the sharp growth in oil revenues as a result of the crisis, overall the proportion of GDP accounted for by the non-oil sector was 54.7 per cent, down from around 62 per cent the previous year.

Progress continued in 1991, with GDP dropping by 0.2 per cent to Dh124.4 billion, due to a decline in oil prices, but the non-oil sector of the GDP continuing to rise, up by 4.2 per cent to Dh71.7 billion, or 57.2 per cent of the total.

Of this, agriculture and fisheries recorded an 8.6 per cent rise over the previous year, water and electricity was up by 7.7 per cent, transport, warehousing and communications by 7.8 per cent, financial services up by 5 per cent, property up by 7. 5 per cent, and construction up by 5.8 per cent. Wholesale and retail trade rose by 4.9 per cent, despite the impact on the economy of the war earlier in the year.

The non-oil sector, according to preliminary figures, continued to make further growth during the course of 1992, and with low oil prices likely to continue for several years, the non-oil sector of GDP should continue to grow both overall and in percentage terms.

confidence to the banking sector, and enabling banks to overcome the negative effects (of the crisis), and regain their role in ensuring liquidity in the national economy."

Confidence was restored, too, across the whole of the economy, and by the end of 1992, it was clear that the country as a whole, and Abu Dhabi in particular, was headed for a further period of substantial growth.

Of particular importance, though often neglected by observers who concentrate on the role of the country as an oil producer, was the

Infrastructure

The growth has, of course, been varied, and in many sectors, the pump has been primed by Government expenditure.

In every sector, for example, the ready availability of water and electricity has proved crucial, and both these, wholly provided by the Government of Abu Dhabi, at highly subsidised rates, have shown considerable expansion.

In 1980, for example, a total of 2.81 million megawatt hours were generated in the Emirate of Abu Dhabi. By 1986, this had risen to 5.62 million MWH, and by 1990, over 7.8 million MWH were generated. In mid-1992, a Dh6 billion (US \$1.63 billion) contract was signed between the Government of Abu Dhabi and a foreign consortium for the execution of the second stage of the major electricity generation and desalination plant at Taweela, on the coast between Abu Dhabi and Dubai.

When completed, by early 1996, it should increase total electricity generation by over a third, supplying sufficient power for the Emirate until the end of the century.

A further Dh950 million (US \$259 milllon) is also being spent on increasing output in the inland oasis-city of Al Ain and in Abu Dhabi, while other smaller plants have been agreed for the remoter areas outside the main population centres.

Production of water through desalination has also received attention. By the beginning of 1992, for example, the Emirate produced around 120 million gallons of desalinated water a day, mainly from the plants at Taweela and Umm an Nar, just outside Abu Dhabi. The Taweela second phase will add a further 76 million gallons a day, sufficient to meet estimated demand in 1996 with a comfortable surplus, while other plants are being built for towns like Mirfa along the coast.

Internal communications have also received investment. The major roads between the centres of population were completed by the early 1970s, although they have since been subjected to continual upgrading. An important factor in encouraging development, however, has been the expansion of the minor roads in the towns and cities. In 1977, for example, there were 650 kilometres of such roads, rising to 4,163 km in 1983, and continuing to rise to 5,001 km by 1987. By 1990, they had risen to 5,660 km, and by early 1993, the total should have exceeded 6,000 km.

Investment by Government in such infrastructural projects has had the result of stimulating growth

شركة الامارات للسيارات، الموزع الرئيسي لسيارات مرسيدس في ابو ظبي، واحدى شركات مجموعة الفهيم، سجلت قصة نجاح فريدة، فقد بدأت انشطتها قبل اكثر من ٢٥ عاما.

Like so many similar success stories, Emirates Motor Co., the main Mercedes distributor in Abu Dhabi, traces its origins to humble beginnings more than 25 years ago.

elsewhere in the non-oil economy. One area has been in the industrial sector.

Industry

Heavy industry, of course, remains primarily in the Government sector, and is closely tied to the oil and gas industry, and its centres at the Ruwais/Jebel Dhanna complex around 300 km west of Abu Dhabi and adjacent to the Umm an Nar refinery and power plant just off the island of Abu Dhabi. This sector has expanded along with the expansion of the oil industry.

There has, however, been growth in other areas, notably at the Mussafah industrial zone, just outside Abu Dhabi, and in Al Ain's industrial area.

Mussafah was conceived as a centre for light industry and for warehousing as part of a plan by UAE President and Abu Dhabi Ruler Sheikh Zayed to make the island-city of Abu Dhabi itself as free as possible from pollution. Long a centre for the automobile industry, it has now other light industrial plants, producing goods ranging from construction materials to furniture and household fittings.

During the course of 1992, however, a decision was taken to transfer to Mussafah the oil industry supply base previously housed on Sadiyat island, to the east of Abu Dhabi and adjacent to the city's port, Mina Zayed.

The project will take two years to complete, at a cost of several hundred million dirhams, involving the dredging of a new deepwater channel for oil rigs and small cargo vessels, and the building of new accommodation and facilities for the two major companies involved, the National Pipeline Construction Company, NPCC, and ADDCAP, a drilling chemicals manufacturer and supplier. Additional housing in the area will also be required, along with a substantial improvement of the local infrastructure, and when the move is complete, Mussafah will emerge as Abu Dhabi's major non-oil industrial centre.

Inland at Al Ain, progress has been achieved primarily in the construction and agricultural industries, the latter, in particular, managing not only to increase production to meet local demand, but also to begin exports, both of fresh and processed goods.

Business and Trade

A good indication of the health of local business and trade is the issuing of commercial licences by the Municipalities (City Councils), in Abu Dhabi and Al Ain, and here as elsewhere, there has been little slowing down in growth. In 1986, for example, Abu Dhabi issued 13,785 such licences, and Al Ain 5,483. In 1989, the year after the end of the Iraq-Iran War, and the year before the invasion of Kuwait, the total for Abu Dhabi had risen to 31,961 and for Al Ain to 6,745, as local merchants and traders sought to position themselves not only for an expanding local market, but also for the possibility of trade with Iran.

In 1990 the totals continued to rise, despite the invasion of Kuwait, to 35,047 for Abu Dhabi, and 6,872 for Al Ain, while preliminary figures for 1991 showed further development. Both cities witnessed further commercial growth during the course of 1992, and the year-end totals of licences were expected to be substantially up on the previous year.

Another source of evidence about growth comes from foreign trade statistics. In 1989, for example, the Emirate exported goods worth Dh685.8 million, re-exported goods worth Dh1.7 billion, and imported goods worth Dh7.4 billion.

Despite the interruption to maritime traffic caused by the invasion of Kuwait, in 1990, exports rose to Dh761.8 million, re-exports to Dh1.8 billion, and imports to Dh8.75 billion, taking total non-oil trade of the Emirate over Dh10 billion a year to Dh11.31 billion for the first time.

The first half of 1991 recorded total trade worth Dh6.1 billion, well over half of the 1990 total despite the Gulf War, and the year total comfortably exceeded the 1990 figure. The first half of 1992 went on to record dramatic growth, with total trade jumping to Dh8.2 billion, little short of the total figure for 1989 of Dh9.9 billion, and representing Dh663 million of exports, Dh1.9 billion of re-exports and Dh5.7 billion of imports. By the end of the year, another record had been comfortably broken.

A comparison between the figures for the whole of 1989 and the first half of 1992 indicate that the greatest percentage of growth has taken place in the export and re-export sectors, though imports themselves have grown substantial in money terms.

The biggest customers for Abu Dhabi's exports and re-exports are the fast growing markets of the neighbouring states of the Gulf Cooperation Council, with Saudi Arabia, Qatar and Kuwait taking the lion's share, either by land or by feeder services up the Gulf.

Imports, by contrast, come primarily from Japan, the United States, Britain and West Germany, although here too Saudi Arabia and Qatar figure in the top ten for the first half of 1992, along with West Germany, France, Italy, Holland and Switzerland.

Internally, the expansion of trade has been fuelled by a number of major projects undertaken by Government and the oil industry, as well as by private enterprise.

The Taweela power project, for example, and the Al Ain International Airport, due to be opened in late 1993, have each had an effect upon the local economy, while the oil industry, both onshore and offshore, is engaged in a five-year development programme that will not only see an expansion of sustainable production capacity, but the bringing on stream of new fields and other projects that together are worth several hundred million dollars.

For the private sector, the activities of the Department of Social Services and Commercial Buildings in providing several hundred million dirhams in low-interest loans for construction have stimulated investment in property. By the end of 1992, the Department had provided loans for well over 30,000 apartments, many of which it manages for the owners, providing them with a risk-free investment. Low commercial interest rates from the commercial banks, down to 6.5 per cent by September 1992 has further helped to persuade investors to embark upon new projects.

Further fuelling this process has been the continued Government programme of paying handsome sums in compensation to local citizens whose houses have been demolished for development projects. For those not so fortunate, over 10,000 low-cost homes have been provided

Modern container handling equipment ensures Mina Zayed is able to handle cargo quickly and efficiently.

رافعة حاويات حديثة في ميناء زايد الذي اشتهر بسرعة عملياته وكفاءتها.

free, with several thousand new ones already planned. The construction contracts for these projects alone are worth hundreds of millions of dirhams, helping further to stimulate the construction industry, and through it, the rest of the private economy.

Many of these new low-cost homes are now being built out of the main population centres, in new towns like Al Wathba, Mirfa and Shahama, for example, generating new centres of economic activity.

Many of the buildings of up to 10 storeys in height that were built in the city in Abu Dhabi's first boom in the late 1970s are now being demolished, to be replaced with others of up to 30 storeys in height, particularly along main streets like the Corniche and Sheikh Hamdan and Sheikh Khalifa Streets. By the end of 1992 a new boom in construction was clearly under way, reflecting the increased confidence in the local market.

Ports

Expanded foreign trade, naturally, has had an impact upon the fortunes of the Emirate's major sea port, at Port (Mina) Zayed, on the outskirts of Abu Dhabi.

Run since the end of 1990 by Sheikh Saeed bin Zayed Al Nahyan, a son of the President, Mina Zayed has long been considered one of the best ports in the Arabian Gulf, with its 21 deepwater berths and extensive container terminal. Patterns of trade and of the international shipping industry for long meant, however, that the port was under-used.

Since the late 1980s, however, there has been considerable growth, which has been particularly impressive since the ending of the Gulf War.

In 1988, for example, the port handled a total container throughput of around 30,000 Twenty-Foot Equivalent Units, TEUs. By 1991, the total had risen to around 45,000 TEUs. In the first half of 1992, however, as the expansion of the Emirate's foreign trade took off, 52,000 TEUs were handled, and by the end of the year, Mina Zayed had achieved a new record for business.

One reason for the upsurge was the changing patterns of the shipping industry. A number of new lines, seeing the opportunity to approach new markets by making use of the port's extensive facilities, started to call for the first time, including Uni Glory, Baltic Shipping and Merzario, shifting away from more congested ports nearer the mouth of the Arabian Gulf.

One benefit was to local traders who began to receive their imports directly through Abu Dhabi, while the port and the economy as a whole also benefited from the emergence of Abu Dhabi as an important transhipment point for goods proceeding to other ports further up the Gulf.

Already at the beginning of the 1990s, a major investment programme had seen Mina Zayed add two new container berths, additional freight sheds and cold storage sheds, and new gantry cranes and straddle carriers.

مطار ابو ظبي الدولي مرفق حديث للغاية يتولى توفير الخدمات لـ ٤٢
شركة طيران عالمية.

Abu Dhabi International Airport is a state-of-the-art
facility serving 42 international airlines.

To be completed by the end of 1993, further investment plans include the purchasing of three new-generation rail-mounted gantry cranes and two yard cranes, a new 20,000-ton cold store, more than doubling existing capacity, more straddle carriers, and the deepening of some of the existing berths to accommodate the latest generation of container vessels.

Shippers and traders are also being enticed with enhanced incentives for the storage of cargo and containers, up to 90 days without charge in some cases.

The operators of the port, the Abu Dhabi Seaports Authority, who also manage the industrial port at Mussafah and the petroleum port at Umm an Nar, are determined that Mina Zayed should play its proper part in the continued development of the Emirate, and results suggest that they are well on the way to achieving that objective.

Aviation

Abu Dhabi's importance in the aviation network of the Gulf and Middle East received a boost from the relocation of the international airport from Bateen to the current state-of-the-art facility, and from the opening in 1987 of the adjoining maintenance operations of the Gulf Aircraft Maintenance Company (GAMCO).

The Dh400 million company, 60 per cent of which is owned by the Government of Abu Dhabi and 40 per cent by Gulf Air, the joint national carrier of the UAE, Qatar, Oman and Bahrain, offers competitive rates to airlines flying between Europe and the Far East as well as to regional carriers.

Many of the 42 international airlines using Abu Dhabi International Airport are now serviced by GAMCO, in addition to the UAE Armed Forces and the Abu Dhabi Aviation Company, which

41

runs a local fleet of helicopters and light aircraft. Based at the capital's Bateen Airport, it provides charter services for the onshore and offshore oil company, ferrying men and material to the oil fields and terminals.

This massive operation, the largest of its kind and most up-to-date in the Middle East, occupies 136 hectares of land adjoining Abu Dhabi International Airport, and is the first in the region to offer aircraft engine and component overhaul.

While GAMCO moves towards international renown in the aviation industry, Abu Dhabi International Airport itself is quickly becoming the gateway between the east and the west. Abu Dhabi's strategic geographic location makes it the ideal transitting point for both regional and international carriers. More airlines are currently negotiating for traffic and landing rights.

Moves are currently underway to add more facilities and amenities at the airport. A key project is the planned opening of a down-town advance check-in and duty free facility which passengers can use up to six hours before their flight. At the airport itself, an additional runway and passenger terminal, a luxury restaurant and a five-star hotel are on the anvil.

Another important aspect of activities at Abu Dhabi International Airport is its general aviation terminal, the home for locally-based Emirates Air Services. A private company, flying fixed-wing aircraft, it has won charter contracts in Yemen for the oil industry, and between Kuwait and Cyprus for the United Nations, in the aftermath of the Gulf War.

Approval has also been received by Emirates Air Services from the Abu Dhabi and Dubai Departments of Civil Aviation for the launching of the first ever shuttle services between the two cities, with other points like Jebel Dhanna, Dalma Island, Al Ain and Fujairah also planned for addition to the service once it starts.

Work is also underway on the construction of the Emirate's second international airport due to open at the end of 1993 in the oasis city of Al Ain, 160 kilometres east of Abu Dhabi. The centre of the Emirate's agricultural belt, Al Ain is also the seat of the Emirates University and has a variety of industries besides being an important stopping point for most tourists.

Agriculture

In an Emirate growing as fast as Abu Dhabi most of its commerce and business is of relatively modern origin. After all, it is only 30 years since the first oil procduction began, while development did not really start until the accession of Sheikh Zayed as Ruler of Abu Dhabi on 6th August, 1966.

There is, however, one sector of the economy that can trace its roots back to the pre-oil era, the traditional pursuits of agriculture, animal husbandry and fisheries.

One of the Government's top priorities has always been the expansion of the agriculture sector, partly to increase output so that the rapidly expanding population is less dependent upon imported food, and partly as a way of contributing to the drive to halt the onward march of the desert sands.

Over the course of the past quarter of a century, thanks to the availability of substantial financial resources, major progress has been achieved.

Lush crops highlight the success of the Government's policies of support for farmers.

Agricultural output has grown rapidly, particularly around Al Ain, where traditional farming has been practised for at least 5,000 years. According to the Al Ain Department of Agriculture, the local marketing centre sold goods worth Dh50 million in 1982, and Dh90 million in the 1985-86 crop year, rising to Dh176 million in the 1989-90 crop year, from over 3,000 farms, covering an area of nearly 250,000 'dunams'.

In the Western Region, covering the rest of the Emirate, the value of vegetables sold in the centre showed an even more remarkable rise in percentage terms, jumping over the three-year period from 1988 to 1990 from Dh13.8 million to Dh47.3 million and the total value of Abu Dhabi's agricultural production has now surpassed Dh250 million a year, excluding all crops grown for private consumption that never come to market.

The variety of crops has grown, too, with onions, potatoes, aubergines, and a mixture of other vegetables being added to traditional staples. To cope with surpluses, a canning factory has been set up in Al Ain which now exports over 50 per cent of its production to the rest of the Arabian Peninsula and elsewhere in the Middle East.

There has been growth, too, in the country's animal wealth.

In 1986, there were 107,000 camels and around 309,000 sheep and goats. By 1990, the number of camels had risen to 142,000, and the number of

تشهد المحاصيل الوفيرة على نجاح جهود حكومة ابو ظبي وسياستها في دعم المزارعين.

sheep and goats to 543,000, while dairy and beef cattle are now being managed successfully in intensive farming units in Al Ain, producing both milk and meat for market.

Demand for chickens and eggs is also being met locally, and again there has been substantial growth. In 1986, 2.25 million chickens were produced for market, and 61 million eggs, while in 1990 2.5 million chickens and 91 million eggs were produced.

Even the fisheries industry is growing, thanks both to soft loans for boats and equipment for the fishermen, and to the setting up of special fishermen's co-operatives that can help both to regulate the industry and to ensure that a proper price is reached in the market.

The new Fish Market in Abu Dhabi, opened in 1992 by the Municipality for the Abu Dhabi Fishermen's Co-Operative Society, handles well over 10,000 tons a year, while the overall catch recorded by the Ministry of Agriculture exceeds 30,000 tons a year.

Together with agriculture and fisheries, both of which have benefited substantially from Government subsidies and investment, there has been remarkable growth too in afforestation.

By the end of 1992, over 12 million palm trees and over 80 million other trees had been planted as a whole in the UAE, the bulk of them in Abu Dhabi Emirate, where over 100,000 hectares have been planted. The date palm crop is now sufficient to make the country one of the world's major date producers, and a new packing plant serves export demand, while other trees bring a benefit of another kind — a dramatic 'greening' of the once desert landscape.

One overall objective of the Government's economic policy over the course of the last 20 years has been to reduce dependence on oil and gas, and to widen the economic alternatives for citizens. Major progress was achieved in the period prior to the Gulf War.

Since then, the firm foundations laid earlier have become a launch-pad for further more rapid progress that is bringing yet more solidly-based and diversified prosperity to both the Emirate of Abu Dhabi and its people.

حققت المزارع التجريبية هدفها المتمثل بزيادة انتاجية المحاصيل.

Experimental farms have also led to an increase in crop production.

4

OIL AND GAS

Over the course of the past 30 years, the pace of development in the Emirate of Abu Dhabi has been dramatic, one that has, in a single generation, changed the country from a poor desert land with a mere subsistence economy into one of modern cities, highways, ports and airports, and of vast expanses of greenery stretching across the once sandy wastes.

The changes never fail to impress first-time visitors, be they humble tourists or world figures like Britain's Queen Elizabeth, former US President Jimmy Carter or France's President Francois Mitterand, for it is a misconception commonly held abroad that Abu Dhabi and the United Arab Emirates are but sand, palm trees, Bedouin tribesmen and camels, along with a few oil wells. The reality is markedly different.

The oil wells, or rather the revenues that have flowed from Abu Dhabi's oil production, have made the development all possible, of course, together with the wisdom and vision of UAE President and Abu Dhabi Ruler Sheikh Zayed, who has ensured that those revenues are put to good use.

In the words of Sheikh Zayed, "Oil is useless if it is not exploited for the welfare of the citizen", and the modern welfare state that the UAE has become owes its very existence to a successful exploitation of oil.

Yet, remarkably, it's no more than 30 years since the first cargo of crude oil was loaded on board a tanker destined for foreign markets.

The story of oil in Abu Dhabi stretches back nearly 60 years, to the early 1930s. The discovery of oil further up the Arabian Gulf, in Bahrain and then in Saudi Arabia, sparked the interest of the major western oil companies in the 1ittle-known Emirates of the lower Gulf, largest of which was, and still is, Abu Dhabi.

The first step was the sending of survey teams

The headquarters of the Abu Dhabi National Oil Company.

46

مقر شركة بترول أبو ظبي الوطنية.

قطاع النفط والغاز

٤

قصة النفط في أبوظبي تعود الى نحو ٥٠ عاماً مضت عندما بدأت الشركات الاجنبية تعمل في التنقيب عن الخام في مناطق متفرقة من الامارة، غير ان القطاع النفطي بدأ مرحلة الازدهار اعتباراً من بداية الخمسينات حيث شهدت أبوظبي تصدير أول شحنة نفطية يوم ٢٦ أكتوبر ١٩٦٢

وخلال السنوات التي سبقت ذلك التاريخ وبعده كانت الشركات الاجنبية تسيطر على هذا القطاع الى ان أمر صاحب السمو الشيخ زايد بن سلطان آل نهيان رئيس دولة الامارات وحاكم أبوظبي بتوطين شركات البترول وبسط السيادة الوطنية عليها.

وكان المرسوم الاميري الصادر عام ١٩٦٩ والقاضي بانشاء دائرة البترول هو الخطوة الاولى للوصول الى الاهداف المنشودة فبهذا المرسوم اصبحت الدائرة اول جهاز حكومي رسمي يشرف على الشركات البترولية العاملة في البلاد.

وتوجت هذه الاجراءات بانشاء شركة بترول ابوظبي الوطنية «أدنوك» التي تحملت مسؤولية استغلال الطاقات النفطية الكامنة في ارض الامارة.

وتمتلك امارة أبوظبي احتياطيات كبيرة من النفط والغاز حيث بلغ الاحتياطي النفطي أكثر من ١٠٠ مليار برميل في حين يبلغ احتياطي الغاز نحو ٢٠٠ مليار قدم مكعب.

وتمشياً مع توجيهات صاحب السمو الشيخ زايد لاقامة صناعة نفطية محلية اقيم مجمع الرويس الصناعي الذي يضم مصفاة طاقتها الانتاجية ١٢٠ الف برميل يومياً ومشروعاً طاقته ٧٥ر٤ مليون طن من غاز البترول سنوياً ومصنعاً للاسمدة الازوتية.

Jack-up rigs stacked in Mina Zayed for the exploration and production which continues apace in Abu Dhabi's prolific offshore fields.

منصة نفطية عائمة راسية في ميناء ابو ظبي استعدادا للمشاركة في عمليات الاستكشاف والانتاج التي تتواصل بدون انقطاع في حقول ابو ظبي البحرية.

out to see if there were any promising surface signs of the presence of oil. One such team from the British-controlled Iraq Petroleum Company arrived in Abu Dhabi in the mid-1930s, and was guided across the desert by Sheikh Zayed, the youngest brother of Sheikh Shakhbut, the Ruler of the day. Archive photographs from that time provide a fascinating insight into the life of the people in the pre-oil era.

Initial signs were promising, and on 11th January, 1939, after several years of negotiation, Sheikh Shakhbut signed a concession with an IPC subsidiary, Petroleum Concessions Limited, covering the whole of the Emirate for a period of 75 years. PCL established its own subsidiary, Petroleum Development (Trucial Coast), PD (TC), to operate this concession, and others elsewhere in what was still known as the Trucial States. Its shareholders included British Petroleum, Shell, Companie Francaise des Petroles — TOTAL, and the American firms that later became EXXON and MOBIL, together with the family firm of Calouste Gulbenkian, the original 'Mr Five Per Cent'.

The outbreak of the Second World War later meant that plans to investigate the concession had to be delayed, and it was not until the late 1940s that PD (TC) began to explore in earnest. Using sturdy vehicles and battling the tough conditions of the trackless desert, the geologists spread out over the land to choose the site for their first well.

The first exploration well, at Ras Sadr, on the coast around 35 kilometres north-east of Abu Dhabi, was drilled in 1950 and was, at the time, the deepest well ever drilled in the Middle East — the first of many records for Abu Dhabi's oil industry. It proved to be a dry hole, as was the second well, but a third at Murban, west of Abu Dhabi and in the heart of the desert, found traces of hydrocarbons. Further drilling ensued, and in 1958, a third well on the Murban structure proved the commercial viability of what was to become known as the Bab field, Abu Dhabi's first oil discovery.

Meanwhile the search had also begun offshore. At the beginning of the 1950s, in what was to prove a landmark decision in international law, Sheikh Shakhbut decided to award a separate concession to cover Abu Dhabi's territorial waters. The first concessionaire, an American firm, declined to follow up the award, and the concession passed to another firm, Abu Dhabi Marine Areas, ADMA, then owned by British Petroleum and CFP-TOTAL, later also to have a Japanese shareholding.

In a little-known but fascinating feature of Abu

منظر في حقل بو حصا البري. والى الادنى مقر شركة جاسكو الذي يقع عند نهاية الكورنيش.

Above: Bu Hasa is one of the onshore fields which have been developed.
Below: The headquarters of GASCO, Abu Dhabi's onshore gas company, is housed in a complex at the far end of the Corniche.

Oil refinery at Ruwais, illuminated by its waste flare and powerful work lights.

مصفاة الرويس النفطية وقد أضاءتها الانوار الكشافة.

Dhabi's oil industry, the great French underwater explorer, Jacques Cousteau, was hired to survey the seabed and recommend a drilling site. He chose well. One of his recommendations was the location for the well that in 1959 discovered the giant Umm Shaif field.

The beginning of Abu Dhabi's oil era

The discovery of the oilfields was merely the first stage. It was followed by a massive construction programme, offshore under the sea, and onshore through dunes and desert, testing man and machine to their limits as new wells were drilled, pipelines laid and terminals built for export, offshore on Das Island and onshore at Jebel Dhanna.

ADMA won the race to complete the task, with the first shipment of oil from Umm Shaif leaving Das in July 1962, and the first shipment of Bab crude leaving Jebel Dhanna in December 1963.

In the 30 years since then the Emirate's oil industry has gone from strength to strength, and in terms of both reserves and production, Abu Dhabi is now up amongst the world leaders.

Onshore, PD (TC), renamed the Abu Dhabi Petroleum Company, ADPC, discovered field after field as its desert explorations continued. The giant Bu Hasa, Asab, Sahil and Shah have all been brought into production, with Jarn Yaphour and Zubbaya (Dhabiyyah), due to come on stream in the next few years. A number of other fields have also been discovered, as exploration continues.

Offshore, ADMA followed up its success with Umm Shaif by discovering another giant field, Zakum, as well as several smaller ones. The planned relinquishment of some of the concession area later saw several other companies either develop ADMA finds, or make their own discoveries. Of these Abu El Bukhoosh, Arzanah, Umm Al Dalkh, Mubarraz and Satah are now in production, with others, like Nasr and Umm Lulu, awaiting development.

As the industry grew, and production expanded, so the political scene changed. Sheikh Zayed succeeded his brother Sheikh Shakhbut as Ruler of Abu Dhabi in August 1966, and in the five years that followed, he and fellow Rulers from the other six Emirates came together to establish the United Arab Emirates, which emerged on the world scene in December 1971.

Over the course of the next few years, the world's

major oil producing countries, among them the UAE, gradually changed their relationship with the major international oil companies, taking control of this key, but depletable, resource.

In Abu Dhabi, this was marked first by the establishment of the Abu Dhabi National Oil Company, ADNOC, in 1971, followed by the signing of participation agreements with the foreign shareholders in ADPC and ADMA that saw the Government's percentage of the concession ownership rise in two stages to 60 per cent by the late 1970s. Onshore, ADPC was replaced by the Abu Dhabi Company for Onshore Oil Operations, ADCO, while offshore ADMA was replaced by the Abu Dhabi Marine Operating Company, ADMA-OPCO, with the same foreign consortia continuing to hold 40 per cent of each firm.

Another major re-structuring took place in the Zakum field, with Lower Zakum staying with ADMA-OPCO, and Upper Zakum being hived off and handed over to a new company, the Zakum Development Company, ZADCO, owned 88 per cent by ADNOC, and 12 per cent by the Japan Oil Development Company, JODCO, which by this time had also bought into the ADMA consortium.

ADNOC and JODCO also jointly developed the small Umm Al Dalkh field, whose well-head towers can be seen on a fine day from Abu Dhabi's Corniche. Other operating firms, in which ADNOC has no percentage share, include TOTAL Abu El Bukhoosh, running the field of the same name, an Amerada Hess consortium running the Arzanah field, and the Abu Dhabi Oil Company of Japan, ADOC, with the Mubarraz and West Mubarraz fields.

One proud boast of Abu Dhabi's oil industry is that its extensive annual exploration programme over the last 30 years has generally meant that new discoveries match or exceed the amount of oil actually produced, meaning that reserves rise year by year. There can be few better guarantees of the Emirate's long-term prosperity.

According to the latest unofficial estimates, total reserves, recently upgraded, now amount to around 200 billion barrels, of which at least 120 billion are recoverable using current techniques, making Abu Dhabi second only to Saudi Arabia, and destined to be a major player in the international oil market for well over a century to come.

Together with the oil discoveries have come finds of natural gas too, some, but by no means all, in association with oil. Industry estimates suggest that Abu Dhabi has a little over 180 trillion cubic feet

منصات حفر عائمة تستعد لمواصلة التنقيب والتطوير في الآبار البحرية.

Jack-up rigs will continue exploration and development of offshore wells in the Gulf.

(5.1 trillion cubic metres) of recoverable gas reserves, larger than any other country except the former Soviet Union, Iran and Saudi Arabia. These reserves too are sufficient to guarantee more than a hundred years of production.

Until the mid-1970s, virtually all of the associated gas from the oilfields was flared off into the atmosphere, creating the eerie night landscape of flames once so familiar to visitors arriving by air, but at the same time wasting a valuable natural resource and polluting the atmosphere.

Since the mid-1970s, however, the Government of Abu Dhabi, acting through ADNOC, has implemented a programme of harnessing the associated gas, rather than wasting it, both for

liquefaction and processing for domestic consumption and export, and for re-injection into the oil-bearing strata to enhance oil recovery.

Under the terms of the oil concession agreements, gas reserves belong wholly to the Government, and in association with its industry partners, ADNOC has established two major companies, Abu Dhabi Gas Industries, GASCO, onshore, and the Abu Dhabi Gas Liquefaction Company, ADGAS, offshore, to process the gas being produced.

GASCO and ADCO produce their gas and oil deep in the desert, from where it flows along a network of pipelines to the industrial zone of Ruwais and Jebel Dhanna, in the far west of the Emirate. Processing takes place mainly at Ruwais, where

The Murban-3 well, pictured here in 1960 proved the commercial viability of the Bab field.

اثبت بئر مربان ـ ٣ الذي يبدو في هذه الصورة الملتقطة عام ١٩٦٠ توفر النفط بكميات تجارية في حقل باب.

there is a hydrocracker unit, a refinery handling well over 125,000 barrels a day of crude, and now more than 10 years old, as well as other units such as the plant of Ruwais Fertiliser Industries, FERTIL, a joint venture between ADNOC and CFP-TOTAL, which produces sulphur, ammonia, urea and other by-products for the local market and for export. Plans to more than double capacity of the Ruwais refinery to 270,000 barrels a day are under consideration, as well as the addition of a condensate production capacity of 120,000 bpd.

ADNOC also operates other plants in the oilfields, at Habshan, for the treatment of non-associated gas, mainly from the Thamama 'F' and 'C' reservoirs, which between them can handle well over 700 million cubic feet (19.8 million cubic metres) a day.

The purified Natural Gas Liquids, NGLs, are split into propane, butane and pentane which, along with the crude oil, are then either exported from the Jebel Dhanna terminal, or fed by pipeline to another industrial centre at Umm an Nar, adjacent to Abu Dhabi island. Here another refinery with a capacity of around 80,000 barrels per day complements the Ruwais refinery to provide the Emirate with an installed refining capacity of over 200,000 bpd, more than double local demand, thus permitting the Emirate to succeed as an exporter of refined products as well as crude oil.

Gas is also fed by pipeline to the inland oasis-city of Al Ain, and overall ADNOC gas pipelines total 575 kilometres on length.

The Umm an Nar refinery is complemented by the plant of National Chlorine Industries, another ADNOC subsidiary, which produces salt, chlorine, caustic soda, hydrochloric acid and sodium hypochlorite, and by a major desalination and power complex, fuelled by products from the oil and gas industry.

Offshore, ADGAS and ADMA-OPCO share the small island of Das, some 250 kilometres north-west of Abu Dhabi, once a haunt only of fishermen and birds, but now another major industrial centre. With new projects under construction to expand capacity, the total population of the island, only a few square kilometres in size, is expected to rise to nearly 10,000 during the course of the next few years.

ADGAS produces Liquefied Natural Gas, LNG, and Liquefied Petroleum Gas, LPG. All of the LNG is exported to Japan under the terms of a contract with the Tokyo Electric Power Company, TEPCO, initially signed for 20 years, but now renewed until well beyond the end of the century, under a contract which required the doubling of the plant's capacity,

تكشف الاساليب الحديثة المستخدمة لاستكشاف النفط أسرار الصحراء

Modern methods of seismic surveying unlock secrets of the deserts.

due to be completed by 1994. Japan is the largest single importer of crude oil from Abu Dhabi, and overall the Emirate supplies the Far Eastern economic giant with over a quarter of its entire energy needs.

Other offshore terminals are on the islands of Zirku, for ZADCO, Arzanah, for Amerada Hess, and Mubarraz, for the Abu Dhabi Oil Company of Japan, ADOC.

Abu Dhabi, through its membership of the United Arab Emirates, is also a member of the Organisation of Petroleum Exporting Countries, and determines its oil production and pricing policy in co-ordination with its OPEC colleagues. Over the past few years, production rates have been around two million barrels a day, although installed sustainable production capacity is 500,000 bpd or so more. By way of comparison, the Emirate of Dubai produces less than 500,000 bpd, and Sharjah and Ras Al Khaimah less than 10,000 bpd each of crude oil, although Sharjah also produces a substantial amount of condensate.

The key objective of pricing policy is to achieve a stable and reasonable level which allows both consuming countries to plan their economies and exporters to secure appropriate levels of income without sudden and dramatic fluctuations.

Now, in preparation for the future, and in accordance with ADNOC directives, ADCO is engaged in a massive programme of Full Field Development of its major fields, which will see several hundred million dollars spent over the course of the next five years. This, in turn, will make it possible to produce at current rates, or more, well into the next century. ADMA-OPCO is also stepping up investment offshore.

Besides holding a controlling shareholding in the major oil and gas operating companies and running the refineries, the state oil company, ADNOC, has grown over the course of the last 20 years to become a diversified international industry giant, one of the world's top 10 oil companies. It is headquartered in a fine office complex at the western end of Abu Dhabi city's Corniche.

Its Exploration and Production Division has the brief of ensuring that the Emirate's territory, both onshore and offshore, is fully surveyed and explored, and that maximum production capacity, in accordance with proper field management, is achieved. It also has its own exploration programme, covering an area of 34,750 sq. kilometres, which was recently rewarded by the discovery of new fields offshore, named IC, IB and Bu Dana, and onshore at Haliba.

Among ADNOC's ancillaries and subsidiaries are its distribution arm, ADNOC for Distribution ADNOC-FOD; the National Petroleum Construction Company, NPCC; the Abu Dhabi National Tanker Company, ADNATCO; National Marine Services; the National Drilling Company, NDC; Abu Dhabi Drilling Chemicals and Products Company, ADDCAP and the Abu Dhabi Petroleum Ports Operating Company, ADPPOC, while it also holds a stake in a refinery and fertiliser plant in Pakistan.

ADNOC reports, in turn, to the Government's Supreme Petroleum Council, established in 1988 to oversee all aspects of the local oil and gas industry. Its Chairman is the Crown Prince of Abu Dhabi, Sheikh Khalifa bin Zayed Al Nahyan, who is also Deputy Supreme Commander of the UAE's Armed Forces.

Since the establishment of ADNOC in 1971, the policy of the Abu Dhabi Government, as laid down by Sheikh Zayed, and now implemented by the SPC, has been to steer the Emirate away from being merely a producer of crude oil to become a producer of refined products, and to use this oil-related industrialisation to stimulate other parts of the industrial economy.

It has also sought to utilise revenues not simply for the development of the country, but also to diversify downstream into the energy-thirsty

Continued exploration and development of oil wells ensures that maximum production capacity is achieved.

consumer markets of Europe, North America and the Far East. For this purpose, a special company has been formed; the International Petroleum Investment Company, IPIC, has been established to look at, and to buy into overseas downstream ventures. Important interests have already been purchased in Spain, while other opportunities are regularly examined.

The oil industry has brought great changes to Abu Dhabi, as any visitor can see. It has witnessed great changes itself, as well. Thousands of men, expatriates and citizens alike, live far out in remote desert locations like Asab and Shah, or on offshore islands and super-complexes like Das and Umm Shaif, working long hours to keep the oil flowing. No longer, however, do they have to suffer the hardships of the early years, when there was no air-conditioning in their camps, or when every barrel of water had to be trucked across the desert or ferried across the sea. Now they live in self-contained oases of luxury, appropriately benefiting directly themselves from the development that they and their predecessors have made possible for the people of Abu Dhabi as a whole.

يضمن التنقيب والتطوير المستمرين لآبار النفط تحقيق أعلى مستويات الإنتاج.

5

BANKING AND FINANCE

In 1959, Abu Dhabi received its very first bank, when the British Bank of the Middle East (BBME) opened a branch there. Today the Emirate has a well-established banking community, including three locally-based banks, branches of many major international banks and at least one world-class investment institution — the Abu Dhabi Investment Authority (ADIA). It is also the headquarters of the Arab Monetary Fund (AMF), whose imposing tower on the Corniche glitters in the evening sunshine.

The presence of the AMF means that financial decisions affecting the whole Arab world are made here. The Arab Bank for Investment in Foreign Trade (ARBIFT) is another pan-Arab financial institution based in Abu Dhabi, and in which the government holds a substantial share. As capital of the federation of the United Arab Emirates, Abu Dhabi also contains the head office of the UAE Central Bank.

As one of the world's foremost oil producers, the underlying strength of Abu Dhabi's economy gives the banking system a sheet anchor despite occasional surface turbulence. At the outbreak of hostilities in August 1990, during the Gulf War, there was a large outflow of funds. Government funds made available to the banking system helped to restore confidence. The result was that, as Central Bank figures show, in the following year, 1991, total bank assets in the UAE rose by 10 per cent, to Dh142 thousand million. Central Bank assets in the same year rose to Dh20.4 thousand million, from Dh17.2 thousand million.

During the '70s and early '80s, the world seemed to be knocking on Abu Dhabi's door. The city, now so green and well-groomed, had for a time the air of a giant building site. Oil revenues led to a hectic construction spree as the authorities struggled to provide the infrastructure, services

The Arab Monetary Fund building stands to the right of the Union National Bank.

٥ القطاع المصرفي

يعود تاريخ العمل المصرفي في أبوظبي الى نحو ١٩ عاماً مضت عندما تم افتتاح البنك البريطاني للشرق الاوسط فرعاً له في الامارة عام ١٩٥٩، ومع مرور السنوات تحولت أبوظبي الى مركز مصرفي إقليمي هام يضم عشرات المصارف المحلية والعربية والدولية.

وقد بدأ هذا التحول السريع في مطلع السبعينات واستمر حتى بداية وهي الفترة التي شهدت تضاعف عائدات صادرات النفط ونمو مختلف القطاعات الاقتصادية.

وبالاضافة الى تدفق العديد من المصارف الاجنبية الى البلاد وافتتاح فروع لها في مختلف انحاء الامارة فقد كان من أبرز التطورات التي شهدها القطاع المصرفي في أبوظبي تأسيس عدد من البنوك المحلية التي تمكنت من اثبات وجودها والتوسع في سوق تتميز بالمنافسة الحادة.

ولعبت المصارف التجارية دوراً رئيسياً في عملية التنمية الاقتصادية في أبوظبي من خلال تمويلها لعمليات الاستيراد والتصدير ومشاريع التشييد والبناء والمشاريع الصناعية والزراعية، وكان للبنوك الوطنية مثل بنك أبوظبي الوطني وبنك أبوظبي التجاري نشاط بارز في هذا المجال.

وفي اطار دعم وتطوير القطاع المصرفي وتعزيز قدرات المصارف المحلية شهد عام ٨٥ اندماج ٣ بنوك وطنية في امارة أبوظبي هي بنك الخليج التجاري وبنك الامارات التجاري والبنك الاتحادي التجاري ونتج عن هذا الاندماج بنك واحد كبير هو بنك أبوظبي التجاري.

وعلى مدى السنوات الماضية قامت السلطات المسؤولة ممثلة بمصرف الامارات المركزي باتخاذ العديد من الاجراءات الهادفة الى دعم هذا القطاع الاقتصادي الهام.

مبنى صندوق النقد العربي والى جانبه مبنى بنك الاتحاد الوطني.

and accommodation consonant with Abu Dhabi's new position as the capital of an oil-rich federation.

Multi-million dirham deals were common as businessmen from all over the globe jockeyed for contracts. To meet their financial needs, international banks came in droves, while in addition numerous local banks grew up. By 1980, over 50 banks had a presence in the UAE.

Since those days there has been a structural change in the market. Gone are the vast contracts and the vast loans which went with them. The number of banks has fallen, reduced by mergers among local banks and shrinkage among international ones.

The dramatic drop in oil prices in the early '80s coincided with the virtual completion of Abu Dhabi's infrastructure. The financial environment shrank rapidly. A spate of non-performing loans proved a headache for all banks. It became clear that the overbanking which had become an accepted part of the UAE's financial scene could no longer be allowed to continue.

As early as 1981, the problem of foreign bank numbers had been tackled by a measure which reduced the allowance of branches of foreign banks to eight Emirates-wide.

Where local banks were concerned, the Central Bank increasingly encouraged mergers to take place. This was achieved, although not without some heartache. The result is that the total of Abu Dhabi-incorporated commercial banks has been reduced to three.

As the '90s began, the policy of Abu Dhabi's banks followed a world-wide trend in turning to the small depositor, and catering for retail needs. Banks began to offer such facilities as consumer loans at reasonable rates, investment funds designed for the customer with less spare cash to invest, and computerisation, including home banking. All three Abu Dhabi banks have automated their back office procedures, thus saving time both for the customer and the bank, and all have now invested in Automated Teller Machines.

Banks are now offering a special service to a large and possibly untapped section of the local population — its womenfolk. UAE women are often extremely wealthy in their own right, and many of them run their own businesses. Banks have begun to provide counters, and even whole branches, designed solely for women, which not only offer the privacy which many Abu Dhabi women prefer, but also give investment and business management advice.

A further service for the retail customer which is gaining ground not only in Abu Dhabi, but throughout the Islamic world is Islamic banking. Grindlays Bank (now ANZ Grindlays) was the first foreign bank to launch a fund, the Muarraba, which is managed on Islamic principles. This was intended at first for non-resident Pakistanis only, as Grindlays' Pakistani operations follow Islamic practices and precepts. Among local banks, Abu Dhabi Commercial Bank (ADCB) led the way when it introduced its Islamic fund for investors in 1988.

Some Muslim customers prefer to adhere to strict Islamic principles in their financial dealings. Islamic banking avoids the payment and receipt of interest, as this is considered unlawful.

Such funds confer part-ownership on the investor, who then shares in the profit — or loss — of an enterprise. Currency dealing and real estate are regarded as acceptable investments.

The National Bank of Abu Dhabi (NBAD) is the doyen of Abu Dhabi banks. Founded in 1968, it had two principal aims — to act as banker to the Abu Dhabi government and, as a corollary, to provide banking services to the local population. ADIA holds a large slice of equity in the bank.

NBAD continues to hold its own in the league table of Gulf banks. With assets of nearly $7 thousand million at the latest (1991) count, it ranks 7th as the Arab Banking Corporation (ABC) and Gulf International Bank (GIB).

The bank is highly liquid, with over 50 per cent of its assets held in deposits and other balances due from banks. NBAD's overseas operations constitute an important part of its activities. It has subsidiaries in Washington and the United Kingdom, as well as two full branches in London. It also has branches in Paris, Egypt, Sudan, Bahrain and Oman, and a representative office in Sydney, NSW.

The Abu Dhabi Commercial Bank (ADCB), was established in 1985 through the merger of three former Abu Dhabi-based banks. With a paid-up capital of $340 million, and assets of $2.7 thousand million, it more than holds its own on the financial scene.

In the short span of years since it was established, the bank has earned a reputation as a major progressive and forward-looking financial institution within the Emirates. By the end of 1988, it had wiped out all the accumulated losses of its

يتيح النظام المصرفي الاسلامي انجاز العمليات التجارية بما يتفق مع الشريعة الاسلامية.

The Islamic banking system ensures customers can carry out business transactions in accordance with Muslim principles.

يقع مقر شركة أبو ظبي الوطنية للتأمين وغيره من الابنية التي تضم مصارف ومؤسسات مالية مختلفة في قلب أبو ظبي التجاري. (أعلاه وفي الصفحة المقابلة).

Above and opposite: The headquarters of the Abu Dhabi National Insurance Company, and other buildings housing banking and finance offices, in the commercial centre of Abu Dhabi.

former constituent banks, after making adequate provisions for possible loan losses inherited from its three merged banks. The bank has continued to extend its branch network, now totalling 27. This serves the whole of the UAE, and it has the largest ATM network in the Emirates, amounting to 33, according to 1992 estimates.

These are also used by customers of three

foreign banks, and a number of local banks, by special arrangement. ADCB has a full-fledged branch in Bombay.

Bank policy places a strong emphasis on improving services and utilising assets to realise better returns.

Abu Dhabi's third, and youngest, bank, the Union National Bank (UNB), came into being in 1983. The Central Bank, which is a federal body with its headquarters in Abu Dhabi, has played a key role in regulating the banking system. Coming on the scene at a stage when most of the banks had already established themselves (it was formed only in 1981) the Central Bank was frequently faced with the prospect of having to reverse the status quo.

One example of this was the problem of the high overall number of banks which had proliferated. The Central Bank introduced a range of regulatory measures, from a credit risk bureau to stringent reporting requirements, which have made a significant impact on the management and accounting procedures of banks. It also imposed strict limits on bank directors, in the face of much

powerful opposition. It was instrumental in negotiating mergers between banks not only in Abu Dhabi, but throughout the Emirates.

One of its most successful areas is its supervisory department which maintains close scrutiny over bank operations, sending its own attained staff in on a regular basis to examine the books. Banks are not permitted to declare a dividend until the Central Bank has given the go-ahead.

Another important measure was the impetus given by the Central Bank in persuading the banking community to raise provisions to a level which realistically reflects the extent of non-performing loans, and to lay down guidelines for the classification of such loans.

Together Abu Dhabi's banks and the authorities have tackled the problem of non-performing loans with every appearance of success. The other major — and related — problem, which surfaced in the '80s, is the important question of interest payments on overdrafts.

In the case of straight loans, there is a clear distinction between principal and interest. On

يتميز بنك دبي التجاري المحدود وبنك ستاندرد تشارترد بمقريهما
الحديثين في قلب المدينة.

*The Commercial Bank of Dubai Ltd. and Standard
Chartered both have impressive modern offices in
the heart of the city.*

overdrafts, there is some room for argument as to whether interest becomes principal when it is charged to the customer's account. The issue was of real concern to banks, since interest may, over a long period, far exceed the original overdraft facility. This question was the subject of protracted discussions, before being resolved by a decree issued by the President of the UAE, HH Sheikh Zayed bin Sultan Al Nahyan. The decree ruled that the contractual agreement was paramount in any case under dispute. Bankers were relieved that a law on the subject had been put in place.

Abu Dhabi's oil reserves will last well into the next century, and so long as the world needs oil, income from it will continue to accrue. Nevertheless, the government, in its wisdom, is concerned for the future welfare of its people, and a fund intended to safeguard the income of future generations by investing present surpluses, has been set up. Abu Dhabi Investment Authority (ADIA) is the instrument which manages this fund. At first its offices were located in London, but for long Abu Dhabi has been its headquarters and the centre of its activities.

ADIA does not publish figures, so it is not known exactly how great are the funds at its disposal. Even informed guesses range from $20 billion to $40 billion.

Most of ADIA's funds are managed in-house, but up to one-third of the funds may be subcontracted for management by other institutions. In these cases, ADIA keeps a close watch on strategy and tactics. The board meets every two months, when the management reports to it. Policy is specified to the fund managers in some detail, and strict guidelines are laid down. They have instructions not to approach certain areas of investment, such as armaments, for example.

The Authority maintains a low profile internationally, and shuns publicity. Like all reputable pension funds, its investment policy is extremely conservative and low-risk. It is against ADIA policy to hold a major share in any international company, and holdings in the majority of cases stands below 5 per cent.

Most of ADIA's investments are made in the hard currency areas of West Europe, the United States, Japan, Australia and New Zealand, while in the Gulf region, ADIA, on behalf of the government, is part-owner of the two great Gulf financial institutions — Gulf International bank (GIB) and Arab Banking Corporation (ABC), both based in Bahrain.

The Arab Bank for Investment and Trade overlooks the lush gardens of the capital.

يطل مبنى البنك العربي للاستثمار والتجارة على حدائق العاصمة البديعة.

6

THE LEISURE INDUSTRY

Since oil first started flowing from Abu Dhabi territory some three decades ago, there has been a tremendous growth in Western-style sports and leisure activities. This is due not only to the large influx of expatriates but also to the great interest shown by the local population in non-traditional sports.

However, during this same period, largely due to the determination of Sheikh Zayed that the Emirate's youth should not lose touch with their heritage, traditional activities such as falconry, camel racing, dhow sailing and rowing races, have also flourished.

For the expatriate and national alike, the range and quality of sports facilities on offer is the match of anything elsewhere in the world. Add to this, almost perfect weather for outdoor activity nearly eight months of the year and high disposable income and you have the perfect recipe for a booming leisure industry.

Falconry and camel racing have always been linked to the Gulf states. Before oil, the skills involved in these two activities were inseparable from the local people's way of life. Now, both activities have become fully-fledged sports in their own right and arguably more popular than they ever were before.

Camel races are held every Friday in the cooler season. Owners invest considerable time and money in the search for a winning animal and the top camels are as pampered as any race horse. There is much friendly rivalry among owners.

Much of Abu Dhabi's history is linked to the sea and this link is still celebrated on national and religious holidays with picturesque dhow sailing races and rowing boat races within Abu Dhabi bay. Anyone who has never seen a rowing boat race before is in for a special treat. The elongated boats come from all over the Emirates to compete both for the honour of their tribe and for large cash prizes. Each boat is manned by between 70 and 150

Tennis, windsurfing and horse riding represent the variety in sporting activity to be found in Abu Dhabi.

<table>
</table>

٦ | **الترفيه**

قبل ٢٥ عاماً لم تكن في أبوظبي أية مرافق ترفيهية تذكر، وكانت الألعاب الرياضية والترفيهية السائدة هي تلك المرتبطة بتاريخ وتراث أهل البلاد، مثل رحلات الصيد بالصقور والفروسية وسباقات الهجن وسباقات القوارب وصيد الأسماك.

غير أن الوضع اختلف تماما الآن وأصبحت الامارة تعج بالمرافق والانشطة الترفيهية، فبالاضافة الى الأنشطة الترفيهية التقليدية فقد انتشرت في مختلف انحاء الامارة النوادي الرياضية والمراكز الترفيهية ذات التسهيلات المتنوعة.

وتقدم فنادق أبوظبي الفاخرة التي تديرها شركة أبوظبي الوطنية للفنادق تسهيلات ترفيهية ورياضية واسعة تتراوح بين مراكز للرشاقة والصالات الرياضية المغلقة والتنس والاسكواش ورحلات الغوص وصيد الأسماك وركوب الامواج والتزلج على الماء.

وبالاضافة الى النوادي الرياضية هناك النادي السياحي الذي يضم كافة التسهيلات وبه قاعة كبيرة للتزحلق على الجليد. ومن الأنشطة الترفيهية الأخرى في امارة أبوظبي الرحلات الى الصحراء والوديان بالسيارات ذات الدفع بأربع عجلات، في حين يعد التزحلق على الرمال احدث الالعاب الرياضية ومن اكثرها اثارة. وهناك منطقتان في واحة ليوا والعين تصلحان لهذا النوع من الرياضة.

وتوفر المطاعم والنوادي في الفنادق الكثير من البرامج الغنائية والموسيقية والاستعراضية التي تضفي اجواء متميزة على اقامة الزوار وتجعل من زيارتهم الى أبوظبي ذكرى لا تنسى.

تتنوع الرياضات التي تمارس في أبو ظبي الى حد كبير. فهي تتراوح بين التنس وركوب الامواج وسباقات الخيل.

Zayed Sports City provides top facilities for football and major sports events.

توفر مدينة زايد الرياضية ملاعب ممتازة لكرة القدم ولأهم الرياضات الاخرى.

oarsmen, and the preparations and post race celebrations are colourful spectacles of local traditions.

In recent years, longer dhow races from Dubai to Abu Dhabi have become popular. Contrary to most people's predictions, the sailing dhow has not died a natural death and is now enjoying a period of renaissance, albeit for reasons of leisure rather than vital trade. There can be few more thrilling sights than an elegant full-sized boom (as the large trading dhow is known) cresting the waves, its lateen sail proudly billowing.

Modern craft are not neglected, Abu Dhabi has also held its first international powerboat race. The huge crowds that lined the splendid Corniche — a perfect vantage point — suggest a bright future for the sport in the capital.

Thirty years ago, when virtually the only expatriates were those searching for oil, facilities for western sports were virtually nil. But once the oil-inspired economy snowballed, both the Government and private sector were quick to respond to the need for leisure facilities.

Sheikh Zayed gave land and support for the construction of major sports facilities and clubs, and under his patronage major hotel chains were encouraged to set up in Abu Dhabi and provide

يتمتع زوار المدينة على اختلاف اعمارهم بالرياضات المائية.

Watersports are enjoyed by visitors of various ages.

The lush gardens and mooring jetty at the Sheraton Abu Dhabi provide a delightful setting for recreational activities.

تعتبر الحدائق البديعة ورصيف الرسو في شيراتون أبو ظبي مكانا ممتازا للأنشطة الترفيهية.

further facilities aimed primarily at the expatriate market.

Football, as elsewhere in the world, has found particular support among local youth and is played in almost all schools and at an international level.

The participation of the UAE in World Cup finals has given the sport a tremendous boost and the country boasts a thriving league and cup competition in which Abu Dhabi clubs dominate the scene.

The spectacular Zayed Sports City on the Western Road is a measure of Sheikh Zayed's commitment to providing the best facilities for the country's youth, its huge vaulted silhouette housing the latest arena facilities for both football and major sports events of all types.

Similarly impressive architecture graces the two main camel race tracks, one on the island of Abu Dhabi itself and a second near the main road to Al Ain. Land has also been provided for clubs to create their own football, rugby and cricket facilities,

and all the major oil companies have their own impressive facilities for their employees.

For a large number of Abu Dhabians, however, and for the ever-increasing numbers of tourists, most leisure activities are centred around the city's hotels.

The major hotels, mainly managed by prestigious international chains under the direction of the Abu Dhabi National Hotels Company, are all equipped with extensive recreational club facilities and private beaches.

The climate of Abu Dhabi is ideal for outdoor sports of all types, with only a few days in mid-winter being marred by stormy weather. The spring and autumn weather, in particular, provides comfortable temperatures ranging from 20 to 30 degrees Celsius.

Foremost among the watersports, adding colour to the beaches, is windsurfing, which over the past few years has blossomed in popularity. The conditions in Abu Dhabi bay are ideal for the sport. Boards are available for hire, and most of the hotels also have an instructor available. There are two well-established windsurfing clubs which hold regular races.

Traditional forms of sailing are also popular and there are regular cruiser regattas. Smaller dinghy sailing however, has largely been eclipsed by the excitement of the more speedy catamarans, and the popular Hobie cats and Prindles compete with windsurfers for the brightest sails on the beach.

The Inter-Continental Hotel and the Marina Club also have modern marinas resplendent with motor launches and yachts of every description. The sheltered waters and surrounding islands make Abu Dhabi a safe and exciting playground for boat lovers, and during the weekends the water-skiers and fishing enthusiasts take to the seas in droves, while others prefer to explore or picnic on the many islands.

Dhows are available for hire by the half-day, day or evening. Barbecues on a beach are a favourite alternative to a party indoors, and fishing trips in search of the delicious hammour and red snapper or even some fair-sized game fish are an exciting way to spend a weekend.

Many people have their own speedboats for water-skiing in calm inlets or on the lee side of the many islands, and there is also a water-skiing club fully-equipped with a competition boat, slalom course and ski-jumping ramp.

All of the hotel beaches have refreshments available and the Meridien, Sheraton, Hilton, Inter-Continental and Gulf Hotels have full service restaurants at the water's edge.

The centrepiece of all the hotels' recreation clubs are the swimming pools which are slightly heated in mid-winter and during the summer are cooled to a refreshing 28 degrees, the temperature, it has been discovered, that pleases most of the people most of the time. It may seem warm by European standards, but in Abu Dhabi it provides a welcome refreshing dip without jarring the system.

Many hotels also give swimming lessons under the watchful eye of a trained instructor, and there are also scuba diving lessons available which lead to internationally recognised certification such as BSAC (British Sub-Aqua Club) and PADI (Professional Association of Diving).

In a constant battle to outdo each other the recreation clubs offer a bewildering array of sports and leisure opportunities and each year the list grows. Gymnasiums are equipped with state-of-the-art exercise equipment and offer courses of training, ranging from executive fitness to weight loss or body

تقدم الفرق العالمية عروضا موسيقية منتظمة يسعد بها هواة موسيقى البوب.

Top name international bands make regular appearances, to the delight of pop music lovers.

building, all under the supervision of qualified instructors. For relaxation there are also massage parlours, saunas, steam rooms and Jacuzzis.

Professional instruction is also available at various clubs in such diverse activities as aerobics, keep fit, karate, ballet and jazz dance.

One activity not usually offered by hotels is horse

تتوفر في مياه الخليج الدافئة حياة بحرية غنية تجتذب الكثيرين.

Underwater enthusiasts find no end of attractions in the warm sea.

Independent clubs such as the Marina Club offer members unparalleled leisure facilities.

تتيح النوادي الخاصة، مثل نادي المارينا، مرافق ممتازة للاسترخاء والمتعة والمرح.

riding. The Gulf Hotel branched out into this field some years ago and it has become a very popular activity with both experienced riders and novices, particularly children. Again, trained instructors are on hand to give lessons. Many have taken advantage of this facility to learn a sport they might otherwise never have had the opportunity of doing.

Common to nearly all the clubs, at hotels and others besides, is tennis, the perfect social game for all ages. Professional coaching is available and there are many tournaments and competitions for all levels of ability. In the summer it is too hot to play during the day, so all the courts are fitted with floodlights for games in the relative cool of the evening.

Another popular racquet sport, particularly during the summer when it is too hot outside, is squash, played on air-conditioned courts. Once again most of the clubs have resident coaches and there are frequent competitions.

Not all clubs are based in hotels, however. There are many clubs for the different nationalities among the expatriate labour force and larger, better established companies often provide recreational facilities for their employees.

There are also several independent clubs that the general public can apply to join, including one of the oldest established, known as The Club, which is often erroneously referred to as the British Club. Nowadays, there are members of every nationality. There is also the Marina Club which has become

a popular venue for world-class entertainers on tours to the Gulf.

Less expensive to join than either of these two is the well-equipped Tourist Club, which gives its name to the area stretching from the Meridien to the International Hotel. Almost every sporting facility is available including one of the city's two ten-pin bowling alleys. The other is at the Hilton Hotel.

The Tourist Club is managed by the Abu Dhabi National Hotels Company, which also manages the Ice Skating Rink at the Zayed Sports City which is able to accommodate 450 skaters and seat 1,200 spectators. Ice hockey is also played and teams of both local and mostly North American expatriate players regularly do battle on the ice.

Apart from the traditional pursuits of Arabia already mentioned, several new desert terrain activities have grown up recently. Foremost among these is wadi bashing, where motoring enthusiasts head off into the great outdoors in four-wheel drive vehicles to explore desert and mountain wilderness.

Although the name wadi bashing came from the dried river beds or 'wadis' of the Hajar Mountains in the northern Emirates and Oman, the term is now loosely used to refer to any four-wheel drive expedition, whether into the mountains or across desert dunes.

For those who do not want the expense of their own vehicle, the major car hire companies are all well-supplied with four-wheel-drive vehicles which can be hired for a weekend expedition.

Desert safaris are popular outings.

تحظى رحلات السفاري الصحراوية بإقبال كبير.

Traditional Gulf cuisine is featured at the unique Al Safina Restaurant.

يقدم مطعم «السفينة» المبتكر أشهى الاطباق الخليجية.

Novices to the sport are advised always to travel in convoys as it is easy to get stuck in the soft sand and there are no roadside telephones to ring for aid.

With the growth of tourism to the Emirates, a number of companies have started offering guided safaris into the desert. Their trips usually include a barbecue and a night under canvas. These not only have the advantage of an expert guide to seek out the more attractive oases and points of interest, they also work out both cheap and safe.

As a direct offshoot of these desert safaris, a new sport was born: sand skiing. The sand dunes of the Liwa Oasis and the Al Ain region are reputed to be among the tallest in the world, and a pioneering group of French skiers has proved that a lot of fun can be had by skiing and surfing down them, using a four-wheel-drive to ferry the skiers back to the summit. The video film that resulted from the French trip won the Cannes Film Festival award for sport novelty.

A much older and more genteel pursuit is golf. Traditionally, the game here is played on sand; players hit the ball off a piece of astroturf they carry around with them to get as close to the grass game as possible, except, of course, on the compacted sand greens, which are called "browns" for obvious reasons. Plans are afoot, however, to follow the lead of Dubai and build a grass course.

There are many other clubs and societies covering activities from chess to archaeology, rugby to morris dancing. One of the oldest and most active is the Emirates Natural History Group whose programme includes regular talks and outings open to both members and visitors. A full listing of clubs, their activities and contacts can be found in the back of the local *What's On* magazine.

Of course, with all these activities designed to burn off calories, there are myriad opportunities for putting them back on. Restaurants of every description and price range abound and expatriates in general spend a lot of time eating out. Licensed restaurants can be found in all the main hotels covering the complete range from the finest French cuisine to bar snacks and nearly every type of ethnic cooking.

There is also a plethora of high street restaurants providing excellent meals at considerably less than hotel prices. The majority are Asian and Arabic.

One unique Arabic restaurant is the Al Safina, situated on the breakwater. It was converted from a dhow donated by Sheikh Zayed and specialises in traditional Gulf food.

Many hotel restaurants, and some not in hotels, also provide regular entertainment. Musicians and singers usually do a tour of about three months at one venue — time to be enjoyed but not to go stale with audiences. Check *What's On* magazine for the latest information.

Being the capital city, Abu Dhabi regularly attracts top international entertainers to its various venues including the likes of the Russian State Ballet company, the Gipsy Kings and Engelbert Humperdinck. International festivals have also become a popular feature, ranging from Scandinavian to a Rio Carnival, and several such as British Week have become annual events.

The Abu Dhabi Cultural Foundation also has an impressive variety of less commercial events. Situated in the heart of the city, the foundation comprises a research and documentation centre, a library, several exhibition halls for promoting the visual arts and also a theatre for the performing arts. There are also classrooms and a variety of lessons and courses available ranging from oil painting to lute playing, while a regular series of foreign film seasons is held throughout the year.

7

THE WORLD ON DISPLAY

Abu Dhabi's shops offer an array of goods from all over the world in shops that range from luxury boutiques to open-air stalls. Shoppers in Abu Dhabi discover a paradise that combines old and new, typically Oriental souks where traditional handicrafts are haggled over, and the latest electronic wizardry on sale in gleaming marbled shopping malls.

There is the thrill of exploring the department stores, boutiques and open-air stalls, the dizzying variety of the goods on offer, and the discovery that many imported luxury items are available at prices much cheaper than their country of origin.

The Middle Eastern souk or market-place has an ambience uniquely its own, redolent of past civilisations. Like the voyagers of the past, today's travellers can find perfumes, silks, spices and jewellery. Bargaining over prices is customary in the souks, though in the plusher showrooms and boutiques prices are more usually fixed.

The entrance to Abu Dhabi's new souk is at the top end of Sheikh Hamdan Street, where the steps lead up from the pedestrian underpass. This souk extends between Sheikh Hamdan and Sheikh Khalifa Streets, and consists of a broad, open central pedestrian avenue leading into a large main square. On either side is an inter-connected grid of narrow walkways, interspersed with several smaller squares. At the far end, the overhead pedestrian walkway leads to the Old Souk on the opposite side of Sheikh Khalifa Street, extending back almost to the Corniche. This entire area is crammed with small shops, and open stalls selling a fascinating assortment of goods: gold, household appliances, clothes, electrical equipment, perfumes and Arabic artefacts.

The new central souk building is located between Istiqlal and Al Nasr Streets. This beautiful structure, inspired by traditional Islamic architecture, incorporates the best in modern facilities and design. Meat, vegetables and fish will all be available under

٧ اسواق ابو ظبي

اكتسبت أبوظبي على مدى السنوات الماضية سمعة متنامية كمركز تجاري عالمي ساعدها في ذلك امتلاكها لتسهيلات بنية أساسية متطورة وانتهاجها لسياسة الاقتصاد الحر بالاضافة الى الخبرة التجارية الطويلة لمواطنيها.

وهكذا أصبحت اسواقها مركزاً لعقد الصفقات التجارية وبيع وشراء البضائع القادمة من مختلف انحاء العالم، وأصبحت الزيارة الى أبوظبي لا تكتمل دون التجول في الأسواق وشراء مختلف انواع البضائع والسلع.

ولكل من اسواق الامارة طابعه الخاص فهناك اسواق حديثة وأخرى قديمة تنقلك الى الماضي العريق للمنطقة. كما ان هناك العديد من المجمعات التجارية المعروفة.

ويدهش الزائر الى أبوظبي لتعدد اسواقها وتنوع البضائع والسلع المعروضة بها مما يتيح للمتسوقين فرصة اختيار ما يناسبهم غير ان الاجهزة الكهربائية والالكترونية والكاميرات والهدايا والساعات والذهب تأتي في مقدمة أكثر السلع مبيعا نظراً لانخفاض اسعارها لدرجة ان الامارة توصف احياناً بأنها بمثابة سوق حرة مفتوحة.

وتعد الزيارة الى سوق الذهب تجربة فريدة حيث تتلألأ المشغولات الذهبية في الواجهات الزجاجية للمحلات المتراصة بشكل مثير وكذلك الحال بالنسبة لسوق الخضار والفواكه حيث تعرض مختلف أنواع على منصات بشكل انيق يغري بالشراء.

وتزخر أبوظبي ايضاً بالعديد من المجمعات التجارية التي تتعامل بكافة انواع السلع والبضائع.

تتوفر في أسواق أبو ظبي تشكيلة واسعة من البضائع، بما فيا الكتب والثياب.

Abu Dhabi's souks sell a variety of merchandise including books and clothes.

كل شيء يوجد بوفرة، مثل الخضار والفواكه والنظارات والساعات.

Fruit, vegetables, sunglasses and watches galore.

one air-conditioned roof, making the shopper's task a much easier one. Smaller neighbourhood souks are scattered throughout the city, including two arched pavilions on the Mina Road, one overflowing with fruit and vegetables, the other stacked with a collection of household items. Behind them is the carpet souk, open air stalls swathed in colourful carpets in every imaginable pattern. Apart from a few small hand-made rugs from Afghanistan, the carpets here are all machine-made, mass-produced modern copies of traditional styles, imported mainly from Pakistan and Belgium. Acceptable just as long as you realise you are not buying a genuine Oriental carpet.

Visitors to Abu Dhabi's souks take home with them far more than their souvenirs. They find a lasting memory of local colour and atmosphere, a time-honoured way of life that lives on in today's modern cities.

Most of the shops in the capital city are to be found along and between the three main streets: Zayed the Second, Sheikh Hamdan and Sheikh Khalifa Streets, all running parallel to each other and to Abu Dhabi's beautiful Corniche.

For the antique collector, the UAE is an absorbing treasure trove. Most spectacular are the magnificent Arab chests, for long the most prominent piece of furniture in Arab homes in the region. Made of wood and decorated with ornate brass plating, such chests historically were presented to brides by their husbands for storing clothes and jewellery. Many have drawers in the bottom or at the side and some have secret compartments. Genuine old chests are now quite valuable and eagerly sought.

Coffee pots are indispensable to the Arab way of life, and have been since time immemorial. Coffee is served after meals and to every visitor to one's home or place of business. The coffee pot, appropriately, is the emblem on the one-dirham coin. Antique coffee pots are in great demand and can be found in a variety of styles depending on their region of origin, but all have the characteristic long, curved, beak-like spout. An old pot in reasonably good condition can command a high price.

Other popular traditional items are the khanjar, the short-curved knife in an ornate sheath traditionally carried by every male in the region; old rifles, some decorated with silver inlay; falconry accoutrements such as hoods or decorative perches; relics of the pearling industry — the curved knives used by the divers in the past are quite rare — and the prized Gulf pearls which are still found from time to time in local shops.

Typical Bedouin jewellery — heavy, chunky pieces in silver, often combined with semi-precious stones — is strikingly handsome. Bedouin ladies traditionally received their first set when they married: bracelets, necklaces, rings for fingers and toes, belts, ear-rings, medallions and amulets. The

هناك طلب شديد على المصنوعات العربية التقليدية المتوفرة بكثرة والتي يشتريها الزوار كتذكارات، مثل أواني ماء الورد والمباخر.

Traditional Arabic items are popular and readily available as keepsakes. Hand-crafted rose-water sprinklers and incense burners abound.

silver used in making these pieces used to be obtained by melting down Maria Theresa dollars, formerly the universally accepted currency throughout the Gulf.

When budgets won't stretch to antiques, there is a wide range of modern souvenirs and handicrafts to choose from: coffee pots and sets of cups made in traditional style; miniature coffee sets, brass camels, ornate brass and copper etuis hung on long chains which can be used as evening bags; trays and bowls in beaten copper and brass.

The Dana Plaza, Abu Dhabi's first real department store, boasts a fascinating Arabic corner where traditional perfume oils, incense and woods, embroidered abayas (head coverings) and the men's ghutras (fashionable in Europe) worry beads and flowing robes can be found.

The Rotana Mall in the Khalidya area is an exclusive shopping centre, offering a vast array of Western items in and amongst shops with a distinctly Middle Eastern flavour. The city boasts the handicrafts of other nations too. The Falcon Gallery, Wongs, Roro and an assortment of places with names such as Chinese Palace, Koreana and Chinese Exhibition are full of Far Eastern furnishings, household items and objets d'art which are available at very reasonable prices.

توجد في مراكز التسوق المختصة تشكيلة كبيرة من البضائع الغربية.

Exclusive shopping centres offer a wide variety of Western goods.

Gold is an excellent buy, and jewellery shops are legion. Styles range from the ornate traditional to the modern. There are necklaces, bracelets rings and ear-rings. Charms for a chain or bracelet make good gifts or souvenirs and you can find exquisite miniature coffee pots, dhows, khanjars, camels and other typical designs.

Dressmakers will be dazzled by the glittering profusion of gorgeous fabrics — sequinned gauzes, gold-threaded brocades, iridescent silks from Japan, Indian raw silks and flowery organdies.

Colours range from deep rich glowing tones, to delicate pastels and shimmering golds and silvers. The array is endless.

Abu Dhabi is also a good place to rediscover value for money in many international brands of cameras, watches, audio and video equipment and so on. Cassettes and videos are found in abundance and are cheap, though quality cannot always be guaranteed.

There are gift shops selling exquisite crystal, silver, leather goods, china and porcelain figurines imported from all over the world. Bernardaud, Daum, Baccarat, Limoges, Dupont and Christofle are some of the famous names from Europe seen in the glassware, crystal and china in the capital's exclusive boutiques.

Designer names in clothes for women and men are a familiar part of the shopping scene. Yves Saint Laurent, Dior and Nina Ricci from Paris; Hugo Boss from Germany; Giorgio Armani from Italy; Ralph Lauren from America, all are fashion names seen here in luxury boutiques. There are plenty of lower-priced fashions too with Benetton boutiques, British Home Stores operating under a franchise, and scores of shops selling the cool cotton casuals beloved of the Western expatriate community.

Art shops and bookstores often have prints, water-colours or pen and ink drawings of local scenes, many painted by expatriate artists who have found Abu Dhabi and its desert an inspiration. Falcons, camels and the Arab stallion are all popular subject matters. Posters and greeting cards are also widely available.

On the purely practical side, local pharmacies are up-to-date and stock almost any pharmaceutical product as well as toiletries and cosmetics.

Local supermarkets could compete with any in the world and probably offer a greater variety than many, catering as they do to such a large number of nationalities. Locally produced and imported products line the shelves, including, of course, caviar.

The open-air carpet souk is a colourful shopping destination.

For those with a sweet tooth the local sweet shops will prove irresistible. Arab sweets and pastries, made with honey or syrup, spices and crushed pistachio nuts, many of them soaked in rose or orange water or stuffed with cream, come

يزهو سوق السجاد المفتوح ببضاعته الزاهية.

in great variety and are truly delicious.

On a more mundane level, the humble loaf is not forgotten with Spinneys offering a wide selection of different kinds of bread. The Brioche Bakery makes your mouth water with delectable cheese croissants made with butter, and baked goods from La Chaumine on Khalifa Street are both healthful and delicious.

Shopping in Abu Dhabi will definitely leave you well satisfied.

77

DUTY-FREE SHOPPING

No account of shopping facilities in Abu Dhabi can be complete without the inclusion of the popular Duty Free Complex at Abu Dhabi International Airport.

In the last few years the complex has established a reputation envied around the world for low pricing and top service — and has collected several top awards in the process.

The operators realise clearly the importance of duty-free shopping. Whether for the impulsive gift, the deliberately chosen one, or the collector's item, duty-free shopping brings excitement to air travel, relieves the tedium of transit and marks the first welcome to a new destination. Meanwhile, for the operators duty-free shopping is a booming, multi-million dollar industry.

Passengers expect good service and demand top quality, variety and above all, attractive prices on the items in a duty-free shop.

Elsewhere in the world frequent accusations have been made of unreasonable pricing, a cheap supermarket environment, badly-chosen souvenirs, a bad deal in currency charges and so on.

At Abu Dhabi shoppers are never disappointed. The complex has 22 outlets selling everything from groceries to pearls. Leading the way in popularity are gold and electronics. Not surprising for Abu Dhabi maybe, but certainly surprising in the world at large where liquor and tobacco generally lead the field. Other outlets offer cameras, perfumes, toys, watches — both budget-priced and expensive, fashions, leather goods, books and gifts. There's a wide range of jewellery including pearls and a delicatessen to ensure that all needs are catered for. In all some 50,000 items are offered with a constant review of products by operators and plans for more shops in the future.

In September 1986 Abu Dhabi airport led the way by becoming the first in the Gulf to open an Arrivals Duty Free Shop. Now whether it's touchdown or take-off, the airport caters to the traveller's needs, be it a last-minute indulgence or a surprise gift.

The shops have been designed after thorough study of the needs and preferences of passengers. There are no counters or barriers where shoppers have to wait to be served. They can, instead, walk in to the outlets and choose what they want to buy.

This benefits transit passengers in particular who have only 20 minutes between flights to shop and therefore have no time to stand and wait.

The opportunity to shop may be there — but the pressure to buy is not. Passengers are free to browse with no one hustling them to purchase.

The accent from the start has been on service, and nowhere is this more clearly seen than in the pricing policy adopted at the complex.

The Duty Free Complex is among the cheapest in the world. People usually expect Abu Dhabi to be a very expensive place and imagine that the duty-free shop also has extravagant prices. This is not the case.

Prices cannot fluctuate randomly as everything is computerised. All kinds of credit cards and currencies are accepted.

يضفي التسوق من السوق الحرة متعة على السفر الجوي.

Duty-free shopping adds excitement to air travel.

Some items are sold at cost, all part of providing service before profit.

The complex is operated on behalf of the Civil Aviation Department by the Abu Dhabi National Hotels Company. In 1984 a feasibility study was carried out which resulted in a massive, three-stage programme of renovation, expansion and promotion. The operators set out to create an up-to-date shopping environment, relaxed and enjoyable, utilising the best features of duty-free shops East and West.

It seems they succeeded. In 1986 the complex won the Best New Duty Free Shopping Outlet world-wide at the Duty Free Symposium in Cannes and won international recognition with two major marketing oscars in 1986 and 1987, both Frontier Marketing Awards. Also in 1987, the complex won

the American Gold Star for Quality and Efficiency as well as the Best Marketing Campaign (Operator) award, and added, in 1988, runner-up for the same prize.

In 1991 Abu Dhabi Duty Free won another international award for excellence from Time International magazine for its outstanding advertising campaign in 1990/91. ADDF was also awarded, in 1991, 'Best Enterprise in the Gulf' from Gulf News/DHL.

But perhaps the greatest accolade comes from the passengers who vote Abu Dhabi's complex one of the best.

8

ABU DHABI HOTELS

Abu Dhabi's meteoric growth during the 1970s and 1980s led to a dramatic increase in the number of hotels. Each new addition went one better than its predecessors in facilities and services; the established hotels up-graded and expanded in order to compete.

The result has been that the city is now blessed with a range of excellent hotels able to accommodate every taste and pocket.

Abu Dhabi National Hotels Company operates five of the largest hotel properties which are managed by international chains such as Hilton, Inter-Continental, Sheraton and Le Meridien. Companies of this calibre and expertise have established the infrastructure required to attract tourists on the look-out for exotic destinations with all the comfort of home.

Lured by the mystique of Arabia and the guarantee of winter sunshine, tourists return home impressed by the standard of hotel luxury and surprised at the range and variety of holiday opportunities.

The hotels are almost as important to UAE residents as to visitors, offering entertainment, dining, sports and club facilities. Business people visiting Abu Dhabi's bustling business sector are also well catered for. The conference and secretarial services provided by the major hotels are of international standard.

Outside Abu Dhabi city, visitors will also find first class accommodation in the luxury hotels in the oasis city of Al Ain and at Jebel Dhanna, some 250 kilometres west of Abu Dhabi, a favourite spot with city dwellers for a weekend retreat.

In this final chapter we introduce several leading hotels in Abu Dhabi which are representative of the high standards to be found throughout the UAE.

Golden sands and clear blue seas are among Abu Dhabi's many attractions.

٨ فنادق أبو ظبي

أدى نمو أبو ظبي الكبير خلال السبعينات والثمانينات الى زيادة هائلة في أعداد فنادقها. وكان من نتيجة ذلك ان المدينة اصبحت تضم مجموعة من الفنادق الممتازة التي ترضي كل الاذواق والميزانيات.

وتقوم شركة أبو ظبي الوطنية للفنادق بتشغيل خمسة من أكبر فنادق العاصمة التي تديرها شركات دولية، مثل هياتون وإنتركونتيننتال وشيراتون وميريديان. وقد أدت الخبرة العريضة لهذه الشركات الى تثبيت البنية الاساسية الضرورية لاجتذاب السياح.

ومن المؤكد ان زوار أبو ظبي يعودون الى اوطانهم بأفضل الانطباعات عن سحر الصحراء العربية وشمس شتائها الدافئة ومستوى فنادقها الرفيع والفرص العديدة التي تتاح لهم لقضاء عطلة لا تنسى.

والفنادق في دولة الامارات مهمة بالنسبة للمقيمين فيها بقدر ما هي مهمة بالنسبة للزوار. فهي توفر برامج التسلية والمطاعم الفاخرة والمرافق الرياضية. كما انها تؤمِّن لرجال الاعمال الزائرين خدمات شاملة تشمل السكرتاريا وقاعات المؤتمرات وغيرها.

ولا يقتصر وجود فنادق الدرجة الاولى على أبو ظبي. فهناك عدد منها في العين وجبل الظنة، حيث يقصدهما العديد من الزوار، خاصة خلال العطلة الاسبوعية.

وسنقدم في هذا الفصل عددا من الفنادق الرئيسة في أبو ظبي، والتي المستوى الرفيع لمختلف فنادق الامارات العربية المتحدة.

الرمال الذهبية والسماء الصافية الزرقاء اثنان من مزايا أبو ظبي العديدة.

ABU DHABI GULF HOTEL

The Abu Dhabi Gulf Hotel combines a warm, congenial atmosphere with a wide range of superb recreational facilities, making it an ideal family resort hotel.

Conveniently located near road links to the other Emirates and Gulf countries, the hotel is near the Abu Dhabi International Airport and the Mussafa Industrial Area, yet still only 15 minutes from the centre of town and overlooking its own private beach.

It offers 192 well-appointed rooms and suites and 24 self-catering chalets. Each room is equipped with a private bath and shower, direct-dial telephone, colour TV, individually-controlled air-conditioning units and mini-bar.

Highlighting the resort's beautiful beach and lush gardens is the Palm Beach Leisure Club which features an impressive line-up of sports and recreational facilities.

Set amid tropical palms is the lagoon-shaped temperature-controlled swimming pool with sunken bar and cascading waterfalls. The Health Club boasts a fully-equipped gymnasium, health bar, sauna, massage and jacuzzi. The hotel's riding stables offer lessons for beginners and outings for the more advanced riders.

Other facilities include tennis, squash, 9-hole mini-golf, table tennis, children's playground and various watersports such as water-skiing, windsurfing, sailing and fishing trips.

The hotel holds a number of popular special events each year including the Annual Raft Race and Horse Show, Motorcross Championship, Tennis Tournament, Oktoberfest and the twice-yearly Palm Beach Fiestas.

The Gulf Hotel prides itself on its excellent cuisine. The Palm Beach Restaurant, ideally located on the seafront, is the perfect place to sample fresh seafood and steaks grilled to perfection. Live, romantic music completes the picture and makes for an unforgettable dining experience. The bright and friendly Sheherezade Coffee Shop offers a wide range of Continental and Oriental buffets and à la carte dishes, and Speciality Nights.

The Ranch, a Country and Western bar and restaurant, offers live, foot stompin' music and serves up a tantalising choice of juicy steaks and daily

يحتل الفندق موقعا ممتازا قبالة الشاطيء، وتتوفر فيه اسطبلات خيول ومدربين مختصين (داخل الاطار).

An exotic beach-front location. Inset: The hotel offers riding stables and lessons.

شلال مائي بديع يعلو بركة السباحة في نادي بالم بيتش.

The Palm Beach Leisure Club features cascading waterfalls and a lagoon-shaped swimming pool.

يضم الفندق ٢١٥ غرفة تحيط بها الحدائق والمناظر الخلابة.

Two hundred and fifteen rooms set amidst beautifully landscaped gardens.

sizzlers. The Rababa Nightclub features exotic cabaret shows accompanied by an international band.

Other hotel services include professional sports lessons, free shuttle bus service to and from the city centre, same-day laundry and valet service, car rental, business centre, gift shops and baby-sitting.

The Abu Dhabi Gulf Hotel offers a friendly, relaxing and refreshing alternative to the city's hustle and bustle.

ABU DHABI HILTON

The Abu Dhabi Hilton, surrounded by landscaped tropical gardens and green parks, is located on the Corniche Avenue and is just minutes away from the city centre. Its 200 refurbished rooms with idyllic ocean views boast executive style and quality amenities including a private bath and shower, central air-conditioning, with individual temperature control for maximum comfort, direct international dial telephone, colour TV, in-house movies, radio and wire.

Exclusive to the Executive Floors are a special manager, reception area and staff, private lounge where complimentary drinks and breakfasts are served, multi-function boardroom, secretarial assistance and personalised stationery. Other extras include a robe, hair dryer and scales in the bathroom, hi-fi stereo in each room with an extensive music library.

Gourmets have a fine choice of cuisine in the hotel's many restaurants. There's Continental and Oriental dining in the Pearl which has beautiful views of the surrounding gardens and the Corniche; authentic Japanese delicacies in the Kei Restaurant with sushi, sashimi and tepanyaki counters; traditional Lebanese mezzehs and grills in the Mawal and Cuban-South American dishes at Hemingway's. The L'Express Café, in the lobby, offers a delightful selection of cakes, pastries and savoury dishes, and is an ideal meeting place. For top-class buffets and `a la carte meals, there's the Tarif Restaurant, open for breakfast, lunch and dinner. For after hours, the Safari Discotheque has the latest in music, sound and lighting equipment.

The Hiltonia Sports Club offers superb sports facilities, including three tennis courts, two glass-backed squash courts and an executive fitness centre with relaxing whirlpools, plunge pools and saunas. A temperature-controlled swimming pool is located on the first floor of the hotel. The Hiltonia Beach Club, with its 300 metres of pure white sand, palm groves and flowers, has a sunken bar and restaurant which offers tropical cocktails, light snacks and barbecue dinners. The picnic area has specially imported Bermuda grass and the well-equipped playground for children is constantly supervised.

A variety of watersports is available, including water-skiing, windsurfing, sailing, snorkelling and

يطل فندق هيلتون أبوظبي بحدائقه الغنّاء على الشاطيء البحري الجميل الخاص به. ويتضمن الفندق مرافق عديدة بينها مشرب «سنكن بار» وأربع بركات سباحة متصلة في نادي هيلتونيا بيتش (أعلاه) ومطعم اللؤلؤة ونادي اللياقة البدنية وغرف النوم الفخمة.

The Abu Dhabi Hilton, surrounded by tropical greenery, overlooks its exclusive private beach club. The wide range of facilities includes the sunken bar and four interconnecting pools at the Hiltonia Beach Club (above); Pearl Restaurant; executive fitness centre and luxurious bedrooms.

fishing. Professional instructors are on hand. Guests can opt for pleasure boat trips.

The hotel also provides banquet and conference facilities with highly specialised technical equipment.

THE BEACH HOTEL

Inspired by traditional Arabian hospitality the Beach Hotel makes the most of its stylish and idyllic surroundings. Ideal for business travellers and vacationers alike, it is situated in the heart of Abu Dhabi's business district but with a serene sea-front location which creates the feeling of a resort.

Each of the spacious 254 guest rooms and suites has a private sea-view balcony. With individually controlled air-conditioning, a fully-stocked mini bar and 24 hour room service you can sit back in the

يحتل الفندق موقعاً ممتازاً يطل على البحر، في قلب الحي التجاري لمدينة أبوظبي.

The hotel enjoys a serene sea-front location in the heart of Abu Dhabi's business district.

height of comfort — perhaps choose between the 12 satellite, local and in-house movie channels. Arranged on seven floors in two wings the rooms have the choice of queen, king or twin beds. Non-smoking rooms are also available.

For functions the multi-purpose Al-Diwan Ballroom receives up to 750 people, or can be divided into five smaller rooms depending on the occasion: Meetings for in excess of 450 people, or lunches and dinners for 400. A boardroom style salon is perfect for smaller meetings of around 20.

The hotel's well-equipped Business Centre is located at the lobby level. Facilities include personal computers, laser printers, multi-system VCR, Reuter Monitor Service — all with full secretarial support. Direct dial telephones, fax machines and a voice-mail message service makes telecommunication an easy matter.

At the end of a working day floodlit tennis courts, squash courts and a fitness centre are available for the energetic, with resident coaches to help improve your style. If you prefer relaxation, a massage, sauna and indoor or outdoor Jacuzzi awaits. The outdoor, fresh-water pool with separate children's pool is temperature controlled, while the private beach offers a wide range of watersports. If all this doesn't tempt, golf and other activities can be organised.

The Beach Hotel has a variety of restaurants to choose from: German specialities at the Brauhaus, Come Prima for Italian, or buffets in the spacious, airy Rosebuds. Outdoor refreshments are served at the Beach-Snack, morning coffee or afternoon tea at the Columbia Cafe. Recent additions to the hotel are a Mexican restaurant, Don Pepe, the American bar Fifth Avenue, and Traders Vic's, the world-famous French/Polynesian restaurant.

The Beach Hotel is within walking distance of Abu Dhabi city centre, where you'll find a wealth of shopping areas from traditional souks to haute couture designer boutiques. If you don't wish to leave the comfort of the hotel, a range of shops and services are conveniently located in the lobby and forecourt.

Offering five-star luxury accommodation and facilities to satisfy the most discerning guest, the Beach Hotel invites you to experience and enter "a world of difference".

كل مزايا الفخامة الفريدة والشاملة للنجوم الخمسة هي من العلامات المميزة لفندق الشاطيء.

Five-star ambience and amenities throughout — the trademark of the Beach Hotel.

FORTE GRAND HOTEL

Forte Grand Hotel, Abu Dhabi's newest 31-storey hotel, opened its doors for guests July '93. Situated in the capital city's business centre, the five-star deluxe hotel is built using innovative architectural design which stands out strikingly in the city's skyline.

Of the hotel's 187 rooms, 108 are set aside for Royal Club, a unique personalised service of Forte Grand properties in the region. Upon request, guests occupying one of the Club rooms can have facilities like fax machines, computers, videocassette and compact disc players, complimentary breakfast and beverages served at Al Fanar restaurant, limousine pick-up from the airport, personalised stationery, and a mini safe in each room.

With the business traveller in mind, the rooms are fitted with Voice Mail to ensure no guest misses any message. It is pre-programmed in ten major languages including Arabic, English, French and Japanese.

Non-smokers have not been forgotten either:

أصبح فندق فورتي جراند من العلامات المميزة في مدينة أبوظبي (أعلاه) وتتوفر في جناحه الملكي فخامة لا تضاهى (أدناه).

(Above): A new landmark in the UAE capital. (Below): Enjoy luxury on a regal scale in the Royal Suite.

Two floors are reserved exclusively for non-smokers. Some rooms have specifically been set aside for female guests with feminine toiletries and female staff attending to them.

The hotel has good sports and leisure facilities, too: An indoor pool with Jacuzzi located on the fourth floor adjacent to a compact gymnasium and an exercise area. There is an Olympic-sized outdoor pool, two glass-backed squash courts and a well-equipped gymnasium. Guests can avail of the tennis and beach facilities at the nearby Marina Club.

Of all the facilities offered, the pride of place goes to Al Fanar, the hotel's rooftop revolving restaurant which offers, besides seafood and grilled specialities, a spectacular view of the city's skyline at a height of 120 metres. If your naked eyes do not give you a satisfactory view, there are binoculars ready at hand.

Abu Dhabi's only revolving restaurant, designed by the award-winning Canadian architect Arthur Erikson, takes approximately two hours to make one rotation, so guests have enough time to finish off their meals in case they do not want a repeat view.

The Italian restaurant, Amalfi, promises regular menu changes, thus giving the diner a chance to sample many original dishes and flavours of the country. Adjacent to the restaurant there is a separate dining room for private use of the guests.

The Arabic restaurant offers dishes particular to the Gulf countries while the Brasserie serves food from all over the world. Besides snacks, the Palm Court Victorian Cafe serves 20 different teas and coffees. In the evenings you can enjoy classical music.

With its state-of-the-art communications and entertainment systems, superb location and exceptionally high standards of services and facilities, the Forte Grand Abu Dhabi is your first choice five-star hotel in the capital.

يتميز الفندق بتعدد الخيارات فيه. فمن الممكن مثلا (من الأعلى) تناول الشاي في مقهى بالم كورت ذي الطابع الفيكتوري الانيق، او الاستماع بماكولات مطعم أمالفي الايطالي، او زيارة نادي إيليوجنز الليلي، او تجربة فخامة جناح رجال الأعمال.

The hotel offers a wealth of choice (from top): Tea in the elegant Palm Court Victorian Cafe; the ambience of Italy at the Amalfi restaurant; pulsating rhythms at Illusions; the comforts of an executive suite.

HOLIDAY INN ABU DHABI

At the heart of the city stands the Holiday Inn Abu Dhabi, an imposing 16 storeys etched against the desert skyline.

The hotel, situated within easy reach of the commercial and diplomatic centre, has 283 elegant and spacious rooms and suites with individually controlled air-conditioning and private bathroom. They are equipped with a mini-bar, direct-dial telephone, radio and colour television and free in-house movies.

The Executive Club Bedrooms are stylishly furnished, offering addded comfort and convenience to the business traveller. They feature a mini-bar, hair dryer, trouser press, remote-control colour television, additional telephone facilities, daily newspaper and business magazine. The bedroom adds a touch of luxury to the bathroom with a bathrobe, magnifying mirror, bathroom scales and a selection of quality toiletries.

The hotel features a gift shop, ladies and men's hairdressing salons and a car rental desk located in the lobby.

The rooftop swimming pool provides a peaceful oasis for relaxing in the sun and is served by a pool bar offering light meals and refreshing drinks.

This 'home away from home', is known as one of the best spots in Abu Dhabi for its dining and entertainment. The Al Dana Coffee Shop, open from 5.30am to 11.30pm, serves a large variety of International and Continental dishes and light meals, with breakfast, lunch and dinner daily — buffet or à la carte. Also featured are special theme nights. The Rhapsody Lounge, a good place to unwind, provides a relaxing environment with top-class live entertainment every night.

Café de Paris, sporting the atmosphere of a Parisian Boulevard Café, serves coffee, tea and juices, and delicious cakes and pastries throughout the day and offers takeaways too.

The Western Steak House, a real American steak house, has a unique Country and Western atmosphere. It offers a wide choice of steaks and an impressive salad bar.

The Harvesters is an authentic English country pub, with its wood decor and traditional English beverages and pub grub.

The hotel's comprehensive conference facilities are complemented by a full secretarial service, duplicating and audio-visual equipment.

The fitness room boasts a multi-point bench, jogging carpet, rowing machine and bicycle, and the equipment is available 24 hours daily for enthusiasts.

The superb comfort and friendly service provided by the hotel is synonymous with the reputation of Holiday Inns world-wide.

The Holiday Inn Abu Dhabi was opened in 1980 and is owned by Emirates Property Investments Company, a member of the Al Fahim Group of Companies.

The hotel is the proud recipient of numerous awards, including the Top Ten Torchbearer Award for excellence in product and quality of service in both 1982 and 1983, and the coveted superior service award for many years.

حمام السباحة الموجود على السطح هو واحد من مرافق الفندق الفخمة.

A roof-top swimming pool is just one of the hotel's fine facilities.

The hotel's central location is ideal for businessmen. It offers comfortable executive bedrooms and a wide choice of dining, including the Western Steak House with its unique Country and Western atmosphere.

يحتل الفندق موقعا مثاليا لرجال الاعمال. وتتوفر فيه غرف مريحة، ومطاعم عدة بينها «ويسترن ستيك هاوس» ذو الجو الريفي الغربي.

91

INTER-CONTINENTAL ABU DHABI

The Hotel Inter-Continental Abu Dhabi, recognised as one of the finest hotels in the Emirates, is situated in a prime location, with its own beautiful beach and adjacent to a delightful private marina.

Overlooking the turquoise blue waters of the Gulf and surrounded by lush green gardens, all of the hotel's rooms and suites offer superb views and yet this magnificent hotel is only minutes from the heart of the city and 43 kilometres from Abu Dhabi's International Airport.

As one would expect, the Hotel Inter-Continental offers an excellent variety of dining and entertainment facilities ranging from a Tea Garden style café in the lobby to the well-known fish restaurant, the Fishmarket. Another popular night spot is El Paso, the hotel's Mexican restaurant and cantina, which offers fine cuisine and nightly entertainment. The Pavilion Restaurant has built up a name for itself as the venue for many theme nights and food promotions whereas the Pool Snack Restaurant is popular for light lunches and its wonderful outlook.

Recreational facilities at the Hotel Inter-Continental Abu Dhabi are amongst the most extensive in the Gulf with a fully-equipped gymnasium, saunas and steam rooms, four floodlit tennis courts and three squash courts. A short walk through the marina takes you to one of Abu Dhabi's finest private beaches. Ideal for swimming, water-skiing, sailing, windsurfing or just relaxing in the shade and enjoying the services of the Halfway House snack bar.

The Hotel Inter-Continental Abu Dhabi is the only hotel to have hosted the GCC Summit three times, and in preparation for this important event all the hotel's bedrooms and suites were refurbished during 1992. The result is a truly superb selection of bedrooms and luxurious suites with a refreshingly tasteful decor and all the facilities one would expect from a luxury hotel.

The conference and banqueting facilities are second to none and the hotel is in the unique position of housing two ballrooms, the largest of which is able to host a reception for 1,600 people.

As with the hotel rooms and public areas, both ballrooms and all 10 additional function rooms were refurbished during 1992 in preparation for the GCC Summit.

Conference organisers will be pleased to find that the renovated Auditorium is equipped with the very latest state-of-the-art audio visual equipment including a simultaneous translation system.

Whatever your requirements, be it a formal banquet or a barbecue on a dhow, the Hotel Inter-Continental Abu Dhabi has the ability and facilities to cater to your needs.

Other services available to hotel guests include a well-equipped business centre, airline and car rental desks in the lobby, same-day laundry service and 24-hour room service.

Whether you are visiting Abu Dhabi on business or for pleasure, with an outstanding standard of service and facilities, the Hotel Inter-Continental Abu Dhabi will ensure your stay is enjoyable and memorable.

يضفي الموقع الفريد لفندق أبو ظبي إنتركونتيننتال ومرسى الزوارق العائد له كثيرا من الروعة على شاطئه الخاص ومرفأ الزوارق الفخم. وتتضمن مرافق الفندق مجموعة من المطاعم، وقاعتين للحفلات، وغرفا بالغة الفخامة وركنا للقهوة العربية في ردهة الفندق.

The Inter-Continental Abu Dhabi's private beach makes full use of the hotel's splendid location, including its luxury marina. The hotel facilities include a wide choice of restaurants, two ballrooms, ultra-luxurious accommodation and a welcoming Arabic coffee corner in the lobby.

JAZIRA RESORT

Situated half an hour from Abu Dhabi is the Jazira Resort, the emirate's newest leisure facility. For long family vacations or intimate weekends, the Jazira is your ideal choice. Its relaxed ambience, luxurious interiors, sports and recreation facilities and warm hospitality combine to give you a memorable experience.

The resort enjoys the twin advantages of being within sight of the Abu Dhabi-Dubai highway as well as on the shores of the sea, thanks to a seven-kilometre channel that links its two main parts.

Guests arriving by road are greeted in the main

تجسد قاعة الاستقبال الفسيحة والحديثة طبيعة الفندق بأكمله (الصورة العليا) ويحيط جو مناسب لرجال الأعمال بقاعتي بني ياس والعين (فوق).

The spacious, modern reception area (top) gives a hint of things to come. Above, business-like surroundings of the Baniyas and Al Ain conference rooms.

hotel where 80 superbly equipped rooms and four executive suites are located. However, for the ultimate get-away, there are also 10 two-bedroom and 10 three-bedroom beach-front chalets far from the highway.

A full range of leisure activities are at your disposal, including flood-lit tennis courts, squash, sauna and steam bath, a fully-equipped gymnasi-um, swimming pool and children's pool. A private beach offers excellent facilities for water-skiing, sailing, wind-surfing, fishing and much more.

For the golfer, hotel residents can also make use of the magnificent Emirates Golf Club 18-hole grass course, just 10 minutes away.

The Jazira Resort offers several dining alternatives, from the casual charm of the Bounty traditional English pub and the Safina coffee shop to the Dalma, a delightful restaurant on the beach providing both snacks and a la carte meals.

Conferences, seminars, banquets or receptions

for 10 to 150 people can be accommodated in the Baniyas and Al Ain private rooms, while in the Ghantoot, an elegant and lavishly decorated Arabic majlis, 70 people can be seated in an atmosphere of unmistakeable grandeur.

For anyone looking for those famous bargains of the UAE, the Jazira Resort operates a free regular air-conditioned shuttle coach service to the beautiful souqs of Abu Dhabi and Dubai.

New, exciting and friendly, the Jazira Resort combines an international atmosphere carefully blended with traditional Arab hospitality.

بركة السباحة في منتجع الجزيرة (الصورة الرئيسية). وتبدو في الصورة اليسرى داخل الاطار بوفيه مقهى السفينة. وتفوح رائحة المغامرات البحرية من مشرب باونتي (الصورة العليا). أما مركز اللياقة البدنية (فوق) فهو مكتمل التجهيز.

Poolside at the Jazira Resort (main picture), with the Safina coffee shop buffet (inset left), a hint of seafaring adventure in the Bounty pub (inset top), and the well-appointed fitness centre (inset above).

LE MERIDIEN ABU DHABI

The world comes under one roof at Le Meridien Abu Dhabi, an island of greenery, elegance and beauty that combines the charming and warm hospitality of a self-contained village with the luxuries and amenities of an up-to-the-minute hotel.

Only 30 minutes from Abu Dhabi International Airport in the heart of the prestigious Tourist Club and business area, Le Meridien offers its guests lush gardens and fountains and tropical flowers on the white sand of its private and welcoming beach.

It is a paradise for the businessman who, during the busy week, will appreciate one of the 235 side rooms or suites, all with private balconies from where he can watch the sunset. Le Meridien offers not only accommodation of high quality, comfort and taste, but also caters to its guests' needs for convenience and attention with a complete corporate service including telefax and secretarial assistance.

It is also a paradise for the vacationer and for those who want to tone up their body. The Oasis Recreation Club features magnificent swimming pools with lyrical waterfalls, a stunning beach with water-skiing, windsurfing, sailing and a diving centre with a private instructor. The recreation centre also offers two tennis courts and two squash courts with their own private coaches, and a state-of-the-art gymnasium with instructor and saunas.

Le Meridien has introduced a Health Spa in the grand European tradition. It offers a giant Aquamedic fitness pool, Balneotherapy (intra water massage), jet spray, seaweed applications and bubble-bath system, shiatsu and Swedish massage, a real Turkish bath — and all this in a stress-free environment. The different treatments work together to relieve, relax, tone, nourish and revitalise the body.

Everyone can enjoy the Spa and choose from a variety of treatments ranging from half-an-hour à la carte services to complete six-day (or more) packages. Different types of memberships are available for those who want to indulge in any of these recreational and Spa facilities.

For those seeking a quiet, tropical, lazy day, the hotel offers one of the most refreshing places to be. At the Pool-side Bar you can sip an ice-cooled drink or take a delicious snack during the sunny

The Meridien, a touch of French sophistication with lush gardens, an oasis in the heart of the business area.

قسم اللياقة الصحية الاوروبي ذي القبة الزجاجية.
The grand European Health Spa of the glass dome.

hours, while at the Waka Taua Terrace you can relax with a tropical cocktail and a light snack.

Le Rendezvous Al Finjan is a comfortable meeting place serving light breakfast from 6am and refreshments throughout the day. The perfect setting for a pre-lunch or pre-dinner drink, afternoon tea or just to relax and listen to the piano.

Le Meridien is dedicated to the art of fine food. There is always something to suit every palate. Le Brasserie, with its Café de Paris ambience, is a

يعتبر فندق المريديان بفخامته ذات الطابع الفرنسي وحدائقه الفاتنة، واحة في قلب منطقة الاعمال في المدينة.

خيمة بدوية توفر حفاوة على الطريقة العربية (اعلاه). والى أدنى، مطعم بتروف الانيق الذي يختص بالنكهة الروسية الاصيلة.

Top: A Bedouin Tent offers Arabian style hospitality.
Lower: The exclusive and luxurious Petrov Restaurant reveals a taste of Russia.

مطبخ التندوري الفخم التابع لمطعم المهراجا الهندي.

First class Tandoori cuisine from the Maharaja Indian Restaurant.

gourmet's delight serving casual and refined dishes with a European accent.

The exclusive and luxurious Petrov Restaurant offers a taste of Russia and its delicious cuisine, and if you want to savour first-class Tandoori cuisine, the Maharaja Restaurant is just the place for you.

The Waka Taua, Le Meridien's Polynesian restaurant, serves genuine Far Eastern food in romantic Hawaiian surroundings. The bright and cheery atmosphere makes it an ideal place for a special occasion, whether with an important business client or a loved one. Live music and an early evening happy hour turn a meal into an occasion.

The extremely popular Steak House, where you can just sit back and relax in a casual yet exciting atmosphere, offers a vast array of prime cuts of beef and sauce accompaniments.

Every night is carnival time in the Casa Brasil, with a truly authentic Brazilian feeling where specialities include refreshing cocktails and delicious ice-creams and where the resident band is always a big hit.

The Carousel disco/pub is a unique concept in entertainment and offers a great time out. Dedicated to fun and enjoyment, the Carousel features totally original decor and the latest technology in light and sound. One of the hottest spots in town, it is open from midday to early morning.

SHERATON ABU DHABI

The Sheraton combines all the advantages of a city centre hotel on one side, with superb beach facilities on the other.

Prominently situated on the Abu Dhabi Corniche and overlooking the Gulf, the spectacular Sheraton Hotel Abu Dhabi has twice been voted the best in the AGCC countries. Although it is within walking distance of the city's main commercial district, the hotel sports a beautiful shopping arcade of its own and a range of business services including a well-equipped Business Centre. The hotel has excellent banqueting and conference facilities, including the Arzanah Grand Ballroom with seating capacity for more than 500 people.

In its opulently furnished 255 rooms, hair dryers, scales, mini-safes and bathrobes are standard equipment. Each room also has individually controlled air-conditioning, large comfortable beds, direct-dial telephones, mini-bars, colour TV with in-house movie channels and a selection of both radio and taped music.

The hotel takes particular pride in its quality cuisine and has a wide variety of restaurants specialising in delicacies from all over the world. The Inn of Happiness, voted the best hotel restaurant in the AGCC region, is one of the most authentic Chinese restaurants west of the Great Wall. It serves dishes from Canton, Szechuan, Beijing and Shanghai.

Hojreh, Abu Dhabi's first Persian restaurant, provides a unique setting in which to sample the delights of the traditional cuisine of this ancient culture. For incomparable Italian fare, there's La Mamma, while El Sombrero offers Mexican food to the accompaniment of Country and Western music.

At the Liwa Café there's a choice of buffet breakfast, lunch and dinner and an à la carte menu. And for the fun-loving The Pool and Beach BBQ is featured every Thursday and Friday. The King Creole, a beach-front restaurant, offers delicious Creole food.

The open-air Oriental restaurant, Al Karya, serves Middle Eastern cuisine with an accent on seafood and offers sophisticated Oriental entertainment. The Tavern has the decor and atmosphere of a traditional English pub and is one of the most popular meeting places in town. It is open daily from 12.30pm to midnight and has a variety of special evenings and entertainment.

For nightbirds the rooftop panoramic view offers enjoyable dining with entertainment.

يخيِّم على بارادايز بيتش جو كاريبي رائع.

A Caribbean atmosphere at Paradise Beach.

يجمع الشيراتون كل مزايا فنادق قلب المدينة، مع جميع المرافق المتوقعة في شاطيء بديع.

يوفر الاثاث الفخم للغرف مزيدا من الراحة للضيوف.

Opulently furnished rooms are designed for convenience and comfort.

The Sheraton combines all the advantages of a city centre hotel on one side, with superb resort facilities on the other. The exclusive Paradise Beach has a Caribbean atmosphere and offers endless sports and recreational possibilities, both on and off the water. The hotel has a flotilla of craft from water-ski boats to a 30-foot cruiser, for fishing trips and excursions. Windsurfers, catamarans and sailing dinghies are also available.

There's a modern health club with extensive facilities, including tennis and squash courts and a gymnasium fitted with state-of-the-art exercise equipment. A swimming pool and children's pool set off the top deck of the multi-levelled beach area, overlooked by the shaded snack bar. Outdoor jacuzzis, nicknamed 'Paradise Island', provide a lovely view of the sea and the gardens in the hotel.

PICTURE CREDITS

The flag of the
United Arab Emirates

The location of the UAE within the Gulf

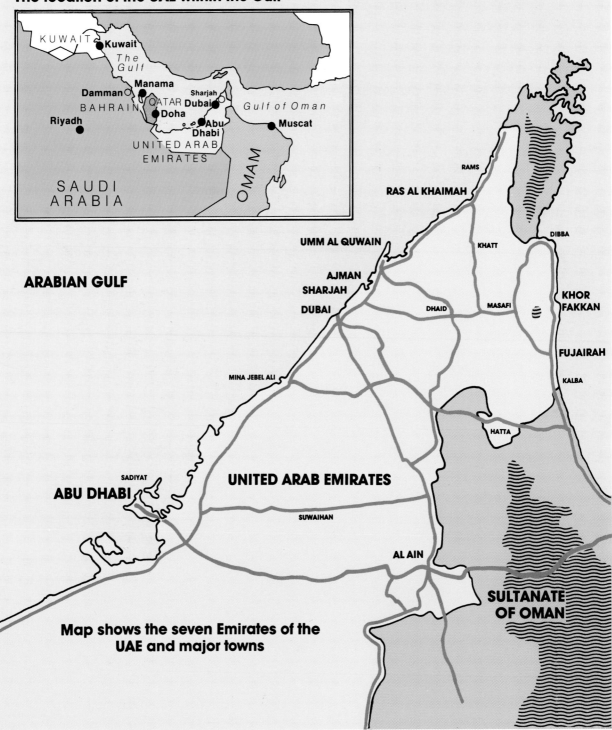

KUWAIT
Kuwait
The Gulf
Manama
Damman
Sharjah
BAHRAIN QATAR Dubai
Doha *Gulf of Oman*
Riyadh Abu Dhabi Muscat
UNITED ARAB
EMIRATES
SAUDI
ARABIA OMAM

ARABIAN GULF

RAMS
RAS AL KHAIMAH
DIBBA
KHATT
UMM AL QUWAIN
AJMAN KHOR
SHARJAH MASAFI FAKKAN
DHAID
DUBAI
FUJAIRAH
KALBA
MINA JEBEL ALI

HATTA

SADIYAT
UNITED ARAB EMIRATES
ABU DHABI
SUWAIHAN SULTANATE
OF OMAN
AL AIN

Map shows the seven Emirates of the
UAE and major towns

INDEX

THE ARABIAN HERITAGE SERIES

Arabian Profiles
edited by Ian Fairservice and Chuck Grieve

Land of the Emirates
by Shirley Kay

Enchanting Oman
by Shirley Kay

Bahrain – Island Heritage
by Shirley Kay

Kuwait – A New Beginning
by Gail Seery

Dubai – Gateway to the Gulf
edited by Ian Fairservice

Abu Dhabi – Garden City of the Gulf
by Peter Hellyer and Ian Fairservice

Sharjah – Heritage and Progress
by Shirley Kay

Fujairah – An Arabian Jewel
by Peter Hellyer

Portrait of Ras Al Khaimah
by Shirley Kay

Gulf Landscapes
by Elizabeth Collas and Andrew Taylor

Birds of Southern Arabia
by Dave Robinson and Adrian Chapman

Falconry and Birds of Prey in the Gulf
by Dr David Remple and Christian Gross

The Living Desert
by Marycke Jongbloed

The Living Seas
by Frances Dipper and Tony Woodward

Mammals of the Southern Gulf
by Christian Gross

Seafarers of the Gulf
by Shirley Kay

Architectural Heritage of the Gulf
by Shirley Kay and Dariush Zandi

Emirates Archaeological Heritage
by Shirley Kay

Sketchbook Arabia
by Margaret Henderson

Juha – Last of the Errant Knights
by Mustapha Kamal,
translated by Jack Briggs

Storm Command
by General Sir Peter de la Billière

Looking for Trouble
by General Sir Peter de la Billière

This Strange Eventful History
by Edward Henderson

Travelling the Sands
by Andrew Taylor

Mother Without a Mask
by Patricia Holton

Zelzelah – A Woman Before Her Time
by Mariam Behnam

The Oasis – Al Ain Memoirs of 'Doctora Latifa'
by Gertrude Dyck

The Wink of the Mona Lisa
by Mohammad Al Murr,
translated by Jack Briggs

Fun in the Emirates
by Aisha Bowers and Leslie P Engelland

Fun in the Gulf
by Aisha Bowers and Leslie P Engelland

Premier Editions

A Day Above Oman
by John Nowell

A Day Above the Emirates
by John Nowell

Forts of Oman
by Walter Dinteman

Land of the Emirates
by Shirley Kay

Abu Dhabi – Garden City of the Gulf
edited by Ian Fairservice and Peter Hellyer

50 Great Curries of India
by Camellia Panjabi

The Thesiger Library

Written and photographed
by Wilfred Thesiger:

Arabian Sands
The Marsh Arabs
Desert, Marsh and Mountain
My Kenya Days
Visions of a Nomad

The Thesiger Collection
a catalogue of photographs
by Wilfred Thesiger

Thesiger's Return
by Peter Clark
with photographs by Wilfred Thesiger

Arabian Heritage Guides

Off-Road in the Emirates
Volumes 1 & 2
by Dariush Zandi

Off-Road in Oman
by Heiner Klein and Rebecca Brickson

Snorkelling and Diving in Oman
by Rod Salm and Robert Baldwin

The Green Guide to the Emirates
by Marycke Jongbloed

Beachcombers' Guide to the Gulf
by Tony Woodward

On Course in the Gulf
by Adrian Flaherty

Spoken Arabic – Step-by-Step
by John Kirkbright

Arabian Albums

Written and photographed
by Ronald Codrai:

Dubai – An Arabian Album
Abu Dhabi – An Arabian Album
The North-East Shaikhdoms –
An Arabian Album
Travels to Oman – An Arabian Album

MOTIVATE
PUBLISHING